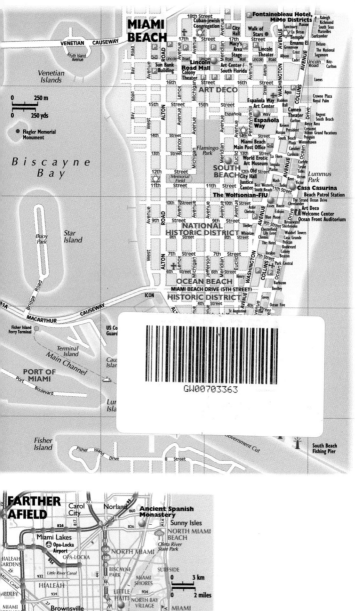

MIAMI BEACH

Fontainebleau Hotel, MiMo Districts

- Cuban-Jewish Congregation
- 18th Street
- City Hall
- 17th Street
- Walk of Stars
- Macy's Area
- 17th Street
- Lincoln Theater
- Sun Bank Building
- Lincoln Road Mall
- Colony Theater
- Art Center / South Florida
- 16th Street

ART DECO
- Española Way Art Center
- Cameo Theater
- **Española Way**
- Miami Beach Main Post Office
- World Erotic Art Museum

SOUTH BEACH
- 12th Old Street
- City Hall
- Justice Center
- **The Wolfsonian-FIU**

NATIONAL HISTORIC DISTRICT
- Art Deco Welcome Center
- Ocean Front Auditorium
- Beach Patrol Station
- Casa Casurina

OCEAN BEACH HISTORIC DISTRICT
- MIAMI BEACH DRIVE (5TH STREET)

Biscayne Bay

Venetian Islands

VENETIAN CAUSEWAY
- South Island Avenue

0 ___ 250 m
0 ___ 250 yds

◆ Flagler Memorial Monument

Buoy Park   *Star Island*

Fisher Island

Fisher Island Ferry Terminal

MACARTHUR CAUSEWAY
ICON

US Coast Guard

Terminal Island
Main Channel

PORT OF MIAMI
Port Boulevard

Fisher Island

South Beach Fishing Pier

Government Cut

FARTHER AFIELD

- Carol City
- Norland
- **Ancient Spanish Monastery**
- Sunny Isles
- **NORTH MIAMI BEACH**
- Miami Lakes
- Opa-Locka Airport
- **OPA-LOCKA**
- **NORTH MIAMI**
- Oleta River State Park
- Little River Canal
- **HIALEAH**
- BISCAYNE PARK
- MIAMI SHORES
- **SURFSIDE**
- **Brownsville**
- LITTLE HAITI
- NORTH BAY VILLAGE
- **MIAMI BEACH**
- VIRGINIA GARDENS
- **DESIGN DISTRICT**
- Miami International Airport
- **MIAMI**
- WEST MIAMI
- **CORAL GABLES**
- Virginia Key
- Hobie Island
- Crandon Park
- Key Biscayne
- **Eco Adventure Kayak and Snorkeling Tours**

0 ___ 3 km
0 ___ 2 miles

GW00703363

CITYPACK TOP 25
Miami

MICK SINCLAIR
ADDITIONAL WRITING BY EMMA STANFORD

If you have any comments
or suggestions for this guide
you can contact the editor at
Citypack@theAA.com

AA Publishing
Find out more about AA Publishing and the wide
range of services the AA provides by visiting our
website at www.theAA.com/travel

How to Use
This Book

KEY TO SYMBOLS

✚ Map reference to the accompanying fold-out map

✉ Address

☎ Telephone number

🕐 Opening/closing times

🍴 Restaurant or café

🚇 Nearest rail station

Ⓜ Nearest Metromover/ MetroRail station

🚌 Nearest bus route

⛴ Nearest riverboat or ferry stop

♿ Facilities for visitors with disabilities

❓ Other practical information

▷ Further information

ℹ Tourist information

✋ Admission charges: Expensive (over $10), Moderate ($5–$10) and Inexpensive ($5 or less)

★ Major Sight ★ Minor Sight

👣 Walks 🚐 Excursions

🏬 Shops

🎵 Entertainment and Nightlife

🍴 Restaurants

This guide is divided into four sections

• **Essential Miami:** An introduction to the city and tips on making the most of your stay.

• **Miami by Area:** We've broken the city into five areas, and recommended the best sights, shops, entertainment venues, nightlife and restaurants in each one. Suggested walks help you to explore on foot.

• **Where to Stay:** The best hotels, whether you're looking for luxury, budget or something in between.

• **Need to Know:** The info you need to make your trip run smoothly, including getting about by public transportation, weather tips, emergency phone numbers and useful websites.

Navigation In the Miami by Area chapter, we've given each area its own color, which is also used on the locator maps throughout the book and the map on the inside front cover.

Maps The fold-out map accompanying this book is a comprehensive street plan of Miami. The grid on this fold-out map is the same as the grid on the locator maps within the book. We've given grid references within the book for each sight and listing.

Contents

Introducing Miami

Sassy, sun-drenched and unapologetically in-your-face, Miami is one sexy city. From the sky-scraping cranes pushing Downtown's skyline to dizzy heights to golden beaches, art deco delights and Latino districts, this is a city on the make and proud of it.

Miami's early pioneers were lured down to the mangrove-lined bay by winter sun, followed by the railroad, which arrived in 1896 en route to Key West. By the 1920s George Merrick had transformed a citrus grove into the elegant Mediterranean-style enclave of Coral Gables, and developers Carl Fisher and John Collins had built causeways across the bay and landscaped a barrier island plantation into Miami Beach. The city's population continued to expand through the art deco revolution of the late 1930s and '40s, the boom years of the 1950s, and Miami's late 20th-century metamorphosis from sunny beach resort to economic powerhouse and influential, bilingual (Spanish/English) "Capital of Latin America."

Exploring Miami's neighborhoods is the key to the city. The world-renowned art deco South Beach (SoBe) district is a must, but it's also fun to drive through Coral Gables, where much of the original "City Beautiful" has survived along lushly tree-shaded streets in one of the city's most prestigious residential areas. Swanky shopping and dining add to its appeal. Coconut Grove now has extensive retail therapy opportunities, but pockets of history still exist here.

For eye-catching evidence of the 1980s building boom and Miami's subsequent upward trajectory, head for Brickell Avenue's condo canyon, extending into the historic Downtown district. Here financial fat cats and political heavyweights rub shoulders with the distinctly Hispanic business district. The spectacular Carnival Center for the Performing Arts, which opened in 2006, flags the route north up Biscayne Boulevard to the Design District, Miami's newest, hippest neighborhood, bordering Little Haiti. Meanwhile, Little Havana buzzes to the west, and east across the causeway Miami Beach beckons.

Facts + Figures

Population: 2.4 million
Ethnicities represented: 150
Languages spoken: 60
Area: 1,955sq miles (3,145sq km)
Government: 35 municipalities

FLOWER POWER

So legend goes, "the mother of Miami," Julia Tuttle, lured developer Henry Flagler south by sending the railroad baron a perfect bouquet of orange blossom in the Great Freeze of 1894–95, when citrus groves farther north had been decimated by frost.

NEW URBANISM

The citywide land use initiative known as Miami 21 will catapult the city into the major league. Integrated residential and commercial development will see the construction of more than 25,000 residential units, 100,000 car parking spaces and four million square feet (370,000sq m) of retail space in Downtown alone over the next few years. Some 100 major building projects have been approved or are currently underway, including a 74-floor tower (the highest building south of New York).

MIAMI AT THE MOVIES

Miami has been a popular movie backdrop for decades. The Marx Brothers (*The Cocoanuts*), Bond (*Dr. No, Live and Let Die, Goldfinger*) and Schwarznegger (*True Lies*) have all starred alongside the city. Ocean Drive shared top billing with Robin Williams (*The Birdcage*), the Miami Seaquarium hosted *Flipper*, and the Hialeah Racecourse flamingoes famously opened the credits for *Miami Vice*.

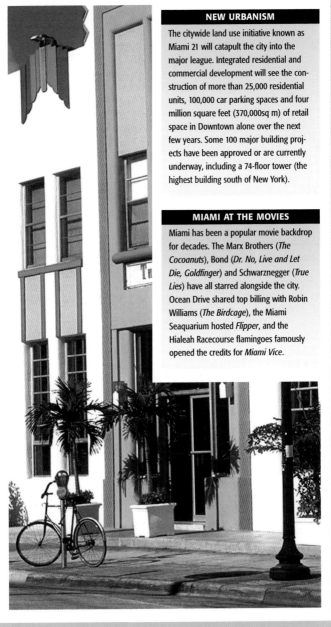

A Short Stay in Miami

DAY 1

Morning If you're staying in South Beach, breakfast at the **News Café** (▷ 56) on Ocean Drive is a local (if rather touristy these days) institution. Even if you're staying farther afield, morning is still the best time to stroll along **Ocean Drive** (▷ 49; Walk, ▷ 54) without the crowds, though you'll still want to return to eyeball the evening parade. The Miami Design Preservation League offers walking tours (Wed–Sun) from their base at 1001 Ocean Drive. Alternatively, visit the **Wolfsonian-FIU** (▷ 50), a few blocks inland from Ocean (the South Beach Local shuttle bus plies a regular route—every 15 to 20 minutes—past the door along Washington Avenue, stopping at Lincoln Road and the Holocaust Memorial).

Lunch Take a break on **Lincoln Road** (▷ 47) for retail therapy and lunch at the **Van Dyke Café** (▷ 58) or have a snack at the **Café at Books & Books** (▷ 59).

Afternoon Continue north past the **Holocaust Memorial** (▷ 46) to the excellent **Bass Museum of Art** (▷ 44–45) and the grand-scale hotels of the **MiMo District** (▷ 52). For something more cutting edge, head across the Julia Tuttle Causeway to the **Design District** (▷ 24–25). Or if the great outdoors beckons, the beachfront **Boardwalk** (▷ 51) unfurls along the sands between 21st Street and 46th Street.

Dinner You haven't done Miami Beach until you've dined at **Joe's Stone Crab** (▷ 60).

Evening The sidewalk tables at **A Fish Called Avalon** (▷ 59) provide a superb ringside seat for people-watching on Ocean Drive. For after-dinner star-gazing (of the earthling variety), try the **Skybar** (▷ 58) before hitting the Miami Beach club scene.

DAY 2

Morning Once you leave Miami Beach, you really do need a car to get around Miami's far-flung districts. South of Downtown, **Vizcaya Museum and Gardens** (▷ 82–83) is a slice of gracious old Miami served up with waterfront gardens and views. It's a great place to recover your equilibrium after a night out on the tiles. If you've got children in tow, try the **Miami Science Museum** (▷ 80), which is just across the street, or take in a couple of shows at the **Miami Seaquarium** (▷ 81) over the Rickenbacker Causeway.

Lunch Coral Way (SW 24th Street) runs west to Coral Gables, past a selection of supermarkets where you can pick up picnic makings for lunch and then enjoy a swim at the **Venetian Pool** (▷ 69), with its Venetian-style lamp posts, cobblestoned bridges and palm trees. Or pop into the **Brasserie Les Halles** (▷ 74) for a *croque monsieur* before strolling past the boutiques and specialty stores of **Miracle Mile** (▷ 71).

Afternoon A drive around the elegant Gables reveals several unusual architectural landmarks, such as the fabulous **Biltmore Hotel** (▷ 64), the **International Villages** (▷ 65) and **Merrick House** (▷ 68). A walk around **Coconut Grove** (▷ 86) is another option, before a sunset cocktail at the bayside **Rusty Pelican** (▷ 90), where you'll get wonderful views across Biscayne Bay to the Downtown skyline.

Dinner Don't leave Miami without going Latino—*the* Cuban restaurant on Little Havana's Calle Ocho (SW 8th Street) is **Versailles** (▷ 40), for succulent roast pork and plantains.

Evening If you're up for a little cha-cha-cha after dinner, try the smoky, sultry cabaret at **Hoy Como Ayer** (▷ 38).

ESSENTIAL MIAMI A SHORT STAY IN MIAMI

Top 25

▶ ▶ ▶

Barnacle Historic State Park ▷ 78 Superbly designed pioneer house in Coconut Grove.

Bass Museum of Art ▷ 44–45 Eclectic art collection in a graceful 1930s building in Miami Beach.

Bill Baggs Cape Florida SRA ▷ 79 State recreation area with Biscayne Bay's best beaches.

The Wolfsonian-FIU ▷ 50 Intriguing design museum in a striking Miami Beach warehouse.

Vizcaya Museum and Gardens ▷ 82–83 James Deering's magnificent neo-Renaissance villa, set in formal gardens.

Venetian Pool ▷ 69 An old quarry transformed into an Italian lido–a perfect place to chill.

South Beach ▷ 48–49 Cosmopolitan, chic and photogenic, this is America's Riviera, packed with art deco gems.

Parrot Jungle Island ▷ 31 Lush gardens, fascinating animals and entertaining shows.

Miami Seaquarium ▷ 81 Dolphins and killer whales keep the crowds entertained, with spectacular shows and side attractions.

Miami Science Museum ▷ 80 Plenty of hands-on exhibits and activities, with a wildlife center and planetarium as well.

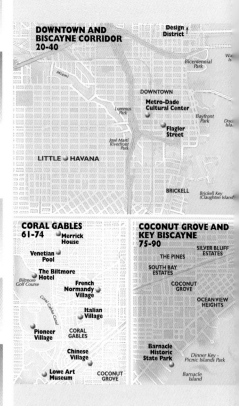

DOWNTOWN AND BISCAYNE CORRIDOR 20–40

Design District

Bicentennial Park

Wa Is

DOWNTOWN

Metro-Dade Cultural Center

Bayfront Park

Dod Isla.

Flagler Street

José Martí Riverfront Park

LITTLE HAVANA

BRICKELL

Brickell Key (Claughton Island)

CORAL GABLES 61–74

Merrick House

Venetian Pool

The Biltmore Hotel

Biltmore Golf Course

French Normandy Village

Italian Village

Pioneer Village

CORAL GABLES

Chinese Village

Lowe Art Museum

COCONUT GROVE

COCONUT GROVE AND KEY BISCAYNE 75–90

THE PINES

SILVER BLUFF ESTATES

SOUTH BAY ESTATES

COCONUT GROVE

OCEAN VIEW HEIGHTS

Barnacle Historic State Park

Dinner Key - Picnic Islands Park

Barnacle Island

Miami Metrozoo ▷ 98–99 One of the top zoos in America, where the animals roam uncaged.

Miami Children's Museum ▷ 30 There's plenty to fire the imagination here.

These pages are a quick guide to the Top 25, which are described in more detail later. Here they are listed alphabetically, and the tinted background shows which area they are in.

The Biltmore Hotel
▷ **64** Still the grande dame of Miami's luxury hotels, now restored.

Biscayne National Park
▷ **94–95** The nation's largest aquatic park and a haven for divers.

Design District ▷ **24–25** ▼▼▼
Dozens of contemporary design stores clustered just north of Downtown.

Fairchild Tropical Botanic Garden ▷ **96**
Take a tram tour around the lakes and tropical trees.

Flagler Street ▷ **26**
The main thoroughfare through Downtown.

Holocaust Memorial
▷ **46** Sculptures and a lily pond in a moving tribute to the victims of genocide.

International Villages
▷ **65** Architectural styles, from French to South African, in Coral Gables.

Lincoln Road Mall ▷ **47**
Attractive open-air mall in the heart of Miami Beach.

Little Havana ▷ **27**
Miami's Cuban district is the place to come for cigars or Cuban sandwiches.

Lowe Art Museum
▷ **66–67** Renaissance and baroque art is the mainstay of this collection at the University.

Metro-Dade Cultural Center ▷ **28–29**
Downtown complex packed with museums.

Merrick House ▷ **68**
The boyhood home of the creator of Coral Gables, restored to 1900s splendor.

Matheson Hammock Park ▷ **97** Acres of shady pathways and a glorious beach.

◀ ◀ ◀

ESSENTIAL MIAMI TOP 25

Shopping

Just like Miami sightseeing, Miami shopping is a neighborhood affair. The city has no central Fifth Avenue or Rodeo Drive, but there are plenty of individual shopping enclaves and malls, offering everything from fashions and vintage clothing to designer furnishing and fabulous kitsch.

Downtown
The waterfront Bayside Marketplace (▷ 32) complex is popular with visitors and combines shopping with live entertainment and international dining. It's a good place to look for souvenirs, T-shirts, fun jewelry and leather items. The Downtown business district around Flagler Street is the nation's second-largest jewelry district and its indoor malls shelter an array of discounted electronics and camera stores. For the most up-to-the-minute Italian-designer furniture, big-name design showrooms and cutting-edge galleries, venture north to the so-hip-it-hurts Design District. On a more prosaic but practical note, the huge Dolphin Mall (▷ 105), out near the airport, is a great place to while away a couple of hours before a late flight if you've space to fill in your suitcase. And way up Biscayne Boulevard in North Miami, the huge Aventura Mall (▷ 105) has plenty to offer.

Miami Beach
There is a small but significant concentration of fashion stores stretched along a two-block strip of Collins Avenue between 6th and 8th streets,

ARTFUL BUYS

In the first week of December, the eyes of the contemporary art and design worlds turn to Miami for the double cultural whammy of Art Basel Miami Beach and Design Miami. Some 200 galleries set up shop in Miami Beach, exhibiting around $2 billion worth of art, while leading design galleries display in the Design District. This is one for serious art and design connoisseurs. However, for more affordable art, check out the Coconut Grove Arts Festival in February.

There are plenty of shopping opportunities in Miami, whatever your tastes and budget

but the most interesting shopping in SoBe is probably found on pedestrianized Lincoln Road (▷ 47), where 12 blocks of galleries, design and clothes stores are attractively interspersed with fountains, sculptures, cafés and restaurants. A cute little Spanish Revival-style shopping street, Espanola Way, still musters a couple of boutiques and galleries, though it is largely given over to restaurants these days. High-end shoppers should make tracks for the Bal Harbour Shops in the Mid-Beach area, where top European designers and Neiman Marcus cater to well-heeled residents and visitors alike.

Coconut Grove

Not quite the shopper's paradise it once was, the Grove is still a fun and easily walkable place to hang out in and explore the boutiques and galleries on Main Highway and Commodore Plaza. The perennially popular outdoor CocoWalk (▷ 87) complex combines shopping, dining and entertainment, and there is more of the same at the Streets of Mayfair (▷ 87), a short walk away.

Coral Gables

On Coral Way, between LeJeune and Douglas, the four-block Miracle Mile shopping district is packed with chic boutiques, bridalwear and specialty stores, galleries and antiques shops. There is also the luscious new Village of Merrick Park (▷ 71), a byword for luxury shopping and just the place to replace your Jimmy Choos after a big night on the dance floor.

BOTÁNICAS

Walk down any shopping street in Little Havana or Little Haiti and you'll soon spot a *botánica*. These little hole-in-the-wall stores are crammed with medicinal herbs (*botánicas*), candles, ceramic saints, balms, beads, relics and mysterious objects used in ceremonies by followers of the Afro-Caribbean voodoo and *Santeria* religions. The stores are an intrinsic part of Miami's Caribbean districts, although they don't exist on the islands.

Shopping by Theme

Whether you're looking for a shopping mall, quirky art gallery or the latest fashion, you'll find it all in Miami. On this page shops are listed by theme. For a more detailed write-up, see the individual listings in Miami by Area.

Miami by Night

Most areas of Miami have their share of restaurants, bars and nightspots, but there are really only two serious contenders vying for the clubbers' crown: the legendary SoBe district on Miami Beach and the city's newest after-dark playground, the 11th Street club corridor at Park West, just north of Downtown, on the mainland.

SoBe

The heart of the art deco district, SoBe is the hang-out of choice for fashion models and glitterati. Take an evening stroll down Ocean Drive and admire the neon-lit hotels, hip diners and excitable crowds spilling out of sidewalk restaurants and poolside bars. The main club scene is on Washington Avenue, while cool bars and lounges are the territory of the Collins Avenue hotels. Popular clubs often have long lines, but it is possible to bypass "the Velvet Rope" if your hotel concierge has connections and can get you into the VIP lounge. For the latest clubbing info, check online or see the listings in the free *Miami New Times*.

Downtown

Fashion is fickle and the hottest clubs in town are currently congregating in the upcoming Park West district on dark pockmarked streets surrounded by building sites. These vast warehouse *danceterias* are loud and sweaty, but if that's not your scene sample earthy blues and cold beer at Tobacco Road (▷ 38), Miami's first licensed premises by the Miami River, or the handful of rather more recherché nightspots in Coconut Grove.

SoBe, with the famous Ocean Drive, is the trendy place to be at night in Miami

CULTURAL HIGHLIGHTS

Hours before the club scene cranks into gear, Miami's cultural venues throw open their doors to welcome theatergoers, music, opera and dance lovers to a veritable feast of performing arts. Art is also on display at the Gables Gallery Night (first Fri of the month), the Design District's Second Saturday and Little Havana's *Viernes Culturales* (last Fri).

Eating Out

Miami is one of the hottest culinary crucibles in the nation. Credited with the invention of Floribbean cuisine—combining New American savvy with exotic Caribbean and Latin American flavors—the city's restaurant scene is bursting with new culinary experiences.

Take Your Pick

Breakfast is served between 7 and 11 and buffets groan under the weight of fresh fruits, cereals, muffins and carb-crazy cooked breakfasts. Lunch (11 to 2) tends to be a salad or sandwich. If you missed breakfast, try a Cuban (ham, pork and cheese stuffed into a loaf). Dinner (6 until late) is the highlight of the day and it pays to be adventurous. Fabulous seafood is a local specialty and there are plenty of Asian-influences at play here, too. Sample Cuban, Argentinian or Peruvian cuisine, and don't forget to down a *mojito* at cocktail hour.

Where to Go

Not surprisingly, SoBe offers the greatest concentration of dining options—and they come in a choice of price ranges. You'll pay a premium to dine on Ocean Drive, but there are several mid-range cafés on Lincoln Road, and affordable diners on side streets. Little Havana is a lively Cuban dining choice, while Coconut Grove's popular bistros and cafés are a good bet, and Coral Gables is considered a gastronomic hub, with prices to match. Dress in Miami is casual, but more formal establishments may frown on blue jeans.

CUBAN CUISINE

Main meals tend to be hearty and filling. Try *sopa de frijoles negros* (black bean soup), *arroz con pollo* (roast chicken with saffron rice), *arroz con camarones* (rice with shrimp), *piccadillo* (spicy ground meat with pimento, olives and raisins) or *palomilla* (thin Cuban steaks). *Tostones* (fried green plantains) or *platanos* (ripe plantains) are popular accompaniments.

Stone crabs (▷ 90, panel); a café on Ocean Drive; Cuban cuisine in Little Havana; Johnny Rockets, home of the burger

Restaurants by Cuisine

There are restaurants to suit all tastes and budgets in Miami. On this page they are listed by cuisine. For a more detailed description of each restaurant, see Miami by Area.

ASIAN-AMERICAN

Grass (▷ 40)

CAFÉS AND BISTROS

Blue Heaven (▷ 106)
Café at Books & Books (▷ 59)
Focaccia (▷ 90)
Greenstreet Café (▷ 90)
Key Lime Pie Heaven (▷ panel, 106)
Van Dyke Café (▷ 60)

CUBAN

Bongo's Cuban Café (▷ 39)
La Carreta (▷ 39)
Larios on the Beach (▷ 60)
Puerto Sagua (▷ 60)
Versailles (▷ 40)

ELEGANT

Azul (▷ 39)
Palme d'Or (▷ 74)

FLORIBBEAN

Ortanique on the Mile (▷ 74)

FRENCH

Le Bouchon du Grove (▷ 90)
Brasserie les Halles (▷ 74)
Chef Innocent at St. Michel (▷ 74)

FUSION

Balans (▷ 59)
Big Pink (▷ 59)
Santo (▷ 60)

HAITIAN

Fidele Seafood (▷ 39)

INDIAN

House of India (▷ 74)

ITALIAN

Caffè Abbracci (▷ 74)
Caffè Milano (▷ 59)
Escopazzo (▷ 60)
Fratelli la Bufala (▷ 60)
Lombardi's Bayside Marketplace (▷ 40)
Osteria del Teatro (▷ 60)

MEDITERRANEAN

Pelican Café (▷ 60)
Perricone's Marketplace and Café (▷ 40)

MEXICAN

El Toro Taco (▷ 106)

MIAMI DINING

11th Street Diner (▷ 59)
Barton G's, The Restaurant (▷ 59)
B.E.D. (▷ panel, 60)
Blue Door (▷ 59)
Chef Allen's (▷ 59)
Michael's Genuine Food and Drink (▷ 40)
Nemo (▷ 60)
Rusty Pelican (▷ 90)

NICARAGUAN

El Novilio (▷ 74)
Guayacan (▷ 40)
Los Ranchos of Bayside (▷ 40)

NUEVO LATINO

Chispa (▷ 74)
OLA at the Sanctuary Hotel (▷ 60)

SEAFOOD

A Fish Called Avalon (▷ 59)
Baleen (▷ 90)
Big Fish (▷ 39)
Crack'd Conch (▷ 106)
Garcia's Seafood Grille (▷ 39)
Joe's Stone Crab (▷ 60)
Monty's Stone Crab Restaurant (▷ 90)
Scotty's Landing (▷ 90)

SPANISH

Casa Juancho (▷ 39)

If You Like...

However you'd like to spend your time in Miami, these top suggestions should help you tailor your ideal visit. Each sight or listing has a fuller write-up in Miami by Area.

PEOPLE-WATCHING

Ocean Drive's sidewalk restaurants and bars offer the best people-watching in town, with Lincoln Road Mall (▷ 47) a close second.
For ringside seats in Coconut Grove, try Greenstreet Café (▷ 90).
Spotting the celebrity guests is all part of the club-scene fun at Mansion (▷ 58).

VINTAGE AND KITSCH

Don't miss Jonathan Adler's fabulously kitsch designer furniture (▷ 56).
Vintage clothing is all the rage in SoBe, so get on down to Recycled Blues (▷ 56).
Fly Boutique is a magnet for vintage-clothing fans (▷ 56).

Shop for "recycled" jeans in SoBe (above), or people-watc from a bar on Ocean Drive (top)

LATIN-AMERICAN CUISINE

The Cuban community vote with their tastebuds and gather at Little Havana's Versailles restaurant (▷ 40).
Brush up on your Spanish for Puerto Sagua (▷ 60).
And then there's OLA (▷ 60). Celebrity chef Doug Rodriguez is Miami's *ceviche* king.

THE LAP OF LUXURY

The Standard's heavenly spa (▷ 111) is the height of relaxation.
The penthouse at the Setai (▷ 112) has its own pool.
Al Capone's suite at the Biltmore (▷ 64) ranges over two floors.

Feast on tasty Cuban dishes at Versailles (above right) or treat yourself to a massage (right) if you feel in need of some pampering

The Freedom Tower, in Downtown

ICONIC BUILDINGS

The Fontainebleau Hotel is a 1950s design classic (▷ 51).

A Downtown landmark, the Freedom Tower (▷ 34) housed the Cuban Refugee Center in the 1960s.

The Atlantis Apartments building (▷ 33) is a 1980s tour de force.

Cesar Pelli's Carnival Center for the Performing Arts (▷ 33) celebrates the rejuvenation of Downtown.

NEON NIGHTS

An evening stroll down Ocean Drive (▷ 49) reveals neon-lit art deco glories.

The Bank of America Tower on International Plaza (▷ 34) themes its illuminations for special events.

***The* spot for sunset drinks,** the terrace at the Rusty Pelican (▷ 90) offers unrivaled views of the Miami skyline.

CLUB CLASSICS

Dance under the stars at Opium Garden and Privé (▷ 58), a sprawling open-air dance club.

Cavernous Downtown warehouse pioneer, Space (▷ 38) caters for the night owls from around 2am.

Clubbing; neon-lit Ocean Drive (above)

PUSHING THE BOAT OUT

Spot celebrity real estate with an Island Queen boat tour (▷ 32).

Rent a kayak at the Bill Baggs Cape Florida SRA (▷ 79).

View the coral reef from a glass-bottomed boat at Biscayne National Park (▷ 94–95).

Relaxing on the sands at Matheson Hammock Park

THE GREAT OUTDOORS

Bird-watch in the Everglades or spot tigers at Miami Metrozoo

Florida's wild side is personified in the vast sawgrass expanses and cypress swamps of the Everglades (▷ 104).

Family-friendly North Shore Open Space Park (▷ 52) is a good place for a picnic and a swim.

Five championship golf courses, including the legendary Greg-Norman-designed Blue Monster, lure golfers to the Doral Golf Resort and Spa (▷ 112).

KIDS' STUFF

There is animal magic aplenty at Miami Metrozoo (▷ 98–99) and Parrot Jungle Island (▷ 31).

The kids won't want to leave the Miami Children's Museum (▷ 30).

Try lizard-spotting in the hardwood hammock at the Barnacle (▷ 78).

WHAT'S FABULOUS AND FREE

A glorious sandy public beachfront stretches 15 miles (24km) from Sunny Isles to South Miami.

Musicians, jugglers, mime artists and more provide free sidewalk entertainment at Bayside Marketplace (▷ 32) from lunchtime until late.

There's no time for sunbathing when there are sandcastles to be built (above)

THE SPORTING LIFE

Local NBA legends Miami HEAT play at the American Airlines Arena (▷ 38).

Paddle a kayak (or canoe) on an eco-adventure tour off Key Biscayne (▷ 84).

Learn to ride a windsurfer at Matheson Hammock Park (▷ 97) and skim the turquoise bay like a bird on the wing.

The American Airlines Arena (right)

Miami by Area

Downtown Miami is being reinvented. Temporarily eclipsed by the rise of Miami Beach and art deco chic, the city's historic seat of government is reclaiming its place center stage and extending its dynamic energy up the Biscayne Corridor to the new club and design districts.

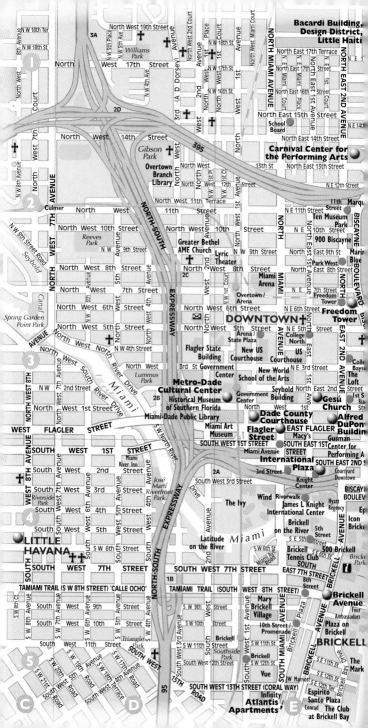

1800 Club
E 18TH ST
Opera Tower

Margaret Pace Park

North Bayshore Drive

...ace
...mni
...chnology
...nter

Doubletree Grand Hotel on Biscayne Bay

...son Miami
...yne Bay
...mi

Biscayne Bay Marriott

Biscayne Island

North   Venetian   Drive

VENETIAN   CAUSEWAY

Venetian Drive

NORTH · BAYSHORE   DRIVE

Herald Plaza

Biscayne C...

Miami Herald Building

MACARTHUR   CAUSEWAY   41

MACARTHUR

Parrot Jungle Island

Bicentennial Park

...centennial Park

Museum Park

Miami Children's Museum

Miami Yacht Club

Ichimura Miami Japan Garden

Miami Outboard Club

CAUSEWAY   A1A

Watson Island

Main Channel

American Airlines Arena

Bayside Marketplace

Miamarina

Boat Tours

Torch of Friendship
...erglades
...the Bay

Hard Rock Cafe

Bayfront Park Amphitheater

PORT   BOULEVARD

Terminal H

Terminal G

P

Terminal F

POM Admin

Terminal E

Seamans Park

P

P

P

Bayfront Park

Challenger Memorial

South End Amphitheater

Dodge Island

P

Seaboard Marine Terminal

PORT OF MIAMI

Terminal J

...ON
...st Union
...nancial Center
...etropolitan
...iami
...AY

Bayfront Park Chopin Plaza

Intercontinental Miami

One Miami

Miami Circle

Tequesta Three

Tequesta One

Brickell Key Drive

Tequesta Two

Brickell Key (Claughton Island)

...reater Miami
...onvention &
...isitors Bureau

Brickell Key Drive

Mandarin Oriental

St Louis

B i s c a y n e   B a y

0		250 m
0		250 yds

F   **G**

Design District

HIGHLIGHTS

- Browsing the design stores
- Lunch at Michael's Genuine Food and Drink (▷ 40)
- Contemporary art at the Moore Space
- Rubell Family Collection

TIP

- On the second Saturday of the month, galleries stay open late, the streets buzz and the place to hang out is the Lounge, a cool bar in the Moore Space.

Miami's Design District originated in the 1920s Land Boom era, when "Pineapple King" Theodore Moore opened a furniture showroom and set about creating a Designers' Row. But this dream seemed long-forgotten when South Beach developer and art collector Craig Robins moved in during the 1990s.

Transformation Robins has almost single-handedly hustled Miami into a position of considerable prominence on the international design scene. He transformed dilapidated warehouses on rundown streets into showrooms attracting cutting-edge designers from around the world and opened up offices, exhibition spaces, galleries, boutiques, restaurants and *ateliers* for young artists. His greatest coup has been to lure the prestigious Swiss

The Design District is home to galleries, boutiques and exhibition spaces. A good place to start is Oak Plaza (bottom right), where you'll find information and a complimentary valet service

design fair Art Basel to host a joint venture, Design Miami and Art Basel Miami Beach, in December.

Explore The hub of the Design District is Oak Plaza. A complimentary valet service and informa-tion are available here, and the main showrooms occupy the grid bound by 39th and 40th streets, between NE 2nd Avenue and North Miami Avenue. The original Moore Building is an exhibi-tion space with frequently changing contemporary art installations displayed in the loftlike Moore Space. Outside, don't miss Enzo Enea's Garden Lounge, a shady bamboo garden with water-lily ponds and seating. If contemporary art is your thing, make a detour south of the Design District to the developing Wynwood Art District, and try to visit the Rubell Family Collection, one of the city's most exciting and extensive modern art collections.

THE BASICS

www.miamidesigndistrict.net
✚ Off map at E1
🕓 Showrooms generally Mon–Fri 9.30–5.30, Sat 10–4
🍴 Restaurants/cafés
🚌 3, 9, 10, 16,
♿ Showrooms free

Rubell Family Collection
www.rubellfamily collection.com
✉ 95 NW 29th Street
☎ 305/573-6090
🕓 Dec–end May Wed–Sun 10–6, 2nd Sat of month 10–10. Closed Jun–end Nov
♿ Moderate

Flagler Street

Gusman Center for the
Performing Arts (left),
in a 1920s theater; a
bus stop mural (right)

THE BASICS

⊞ E3
🍴 Cafés/restaurants
🚌 All buses serving
Downtown
Ⓜ Miami Avenue/
1st Street

HIGHLIGHTS

● Murals of Florida scenes in
the Alfred I DuPont Building
● Gusman Center for the
Performing Arts
● Jewelry dealers in the
Seybold Building, 1st Street
(▷ 36)
● Streetlife

**Crowned with soaring financial bastions
like the Bank of America Tower, glittering
new bayside condo units and the
Freedom Tower, ground-level Downtown
and its main thoroughfare, Flagler Street,
can come as a bit of a shock.**

Latino flair If you were expecting a slick, modern
American business district—all glass, chrome and
short of soul—think again, for Downtown Miami has
more in common with Managua or Caracas. Here,
the bustle and life of a Latin-American street scene
converges with discount stores, jewelry businesses
and gritty building projects. Office workers mingle
with construction crews over Cuban sandwiches
and tiny cups of coffee at lunchtime.

History Flagler Street at Miami Avenue is the
geographic heart of the city grid, from which all
streets are numbered. Nearby, Miami's history
began with a bend in the Miami River where
Tequesta Indians once settled and Henry M.
Flagler built his Royal Palm Hotel some 2,000
years later. Downtown is compact and easily
explored on foot (▷ Walk, 35). Its development
can be traced in a selection of handsome architectural monuments, such as the Spanish-Moorish
style Gusman Center for the Performing Arts
(174 E Flagler), a glorious former picture palace
and vaudeville theater that has hosted the likes of
Elvis and Pavarotti; the Dade County Courthouse
(▷ 34), with its imposing Doric columns; and
the lavishly ornamented Depression-era Alfred I
DuPont Building (▷ 32).

A game of dominoes (left); a mural painting on Calle Ocho (right)

Miami's first wave of Cuban migrants arrived in the 1950s, after fleeing Castro's Communist revolution. They settled in an area of the city just west of Downtown, which was quickly christened "Little Havana."

Calle Ocho Today, some two thirds of the city's population is of Hispanic origin and Little Havana is now home to an increasingly diverse mix of Latin and Central American new arrivals as Cubans move on to more affluent suburbs. The focus of Little Havana is SW 8th Street, better known as Calle Ocho, between 11th and 17th avenues. This is the place to take a stroll, see the few sights that the area has to offer, buy a *guayabera* (a traditional loose-fitting men's shirt), explore a *botánica* (a one-stop shop for Afro-Caribbean religions, from *Santería* to Catholicism, ▷ 11), and sample Cuban specialties, from cigars at El Crédito (▷ 36) to pastries and *café Cubano* at the Exquisito Cafeteria (1510 SW 8th Street).

Domino crazy At the junction with SW 13th Avenue, the Brigade 2506 Memorial commemorates the US-trained Cuban exiles who were killed during the ill-fated Bay of Pigs invasion in 1961. A little farther on at SW 15th Avenue, the rattle of dominoes will tell you that you've reached Máximo Gómez Park, where domino devotees spend the day watching the tumble of the tiles. Interested visitors can watch a while, but this is not an official tourist site and intrusive cameras are not welcomed.

THE BASICS

➕ C4

✉ The focus of Little Havana is SW 8th Street, between 11th and 17th avenues, although the district does spread out farther

🍴 Cafés/restaurants

🚌 8, 12, 17, 208

HIGHLIGHTS

● Watching the deft-fingered *tabaqueros* rolling cigars at the El Crédito Cigar Factory, 1106 SW 8th Street
● Dinner at Versailles (▷ 40), 3555 SW 8th Street
● Buying Latin-American dance records at Casino Records, 1208 SW 8th Street
● Exotic fresh juices from the Pinareños fruit market, 1300 block of SW 8th Street

Metro-Dade Cultural Center

HIGHLIGHTS

Historical Museum
- Hand-sewn Seminole Indian patchwork jacket
- 1925 Miami tram
- Maps of the New World
- Photographs of South Florida pioneer life
- Art deco ornaments
- Prohibition-era exhibits
- Mastodon bones
- Tequesta Indian arrowheads and turtle-shell jewelry
- 16th-century items salvaged from Spanish shipwrecks

Architect Philip Johnson devised this Mediterranean-style setting for the Historical Museum of Southern Florida, Miami Art Museum of Dade County and the Miami-Dade Public Library in 1984.

Historical Museum Spanning indigenous cultures, the Spanish era and the rise of Miami itself, this museum covers the region's past with absorbing exhibits and a wealth of historical objects, as well as outlining the area's ecology. Portrayals of the natural environment flow neatly into exhibits on the lives and lifestyles of the indigenous inhabitants of the area, chiefly the Tequesta people. Numerous items from galleons and early settlements detail the arrival of the Spanish, Florida's first Europeans, whose presence led to the eventual disappearance of the Tequesta.

Clockwise from left: a Seminole Indian costume in the Historical Museum; a tiled fore-court leads up to the library; Spanish items—remnants of the region's colonial past—on display in the Historical Museum; outside Miami Art Museum; and inside one of the galleries; Seminole Indian textiles in the Historical Museum

Not until the 19th century did European settlement gain a lasting foothold in southern Florida, as Key West emerged as a hub for salvaging and cigar production. Meanwhile, the Seminole people—Creek Indians from Georgia who were forced into the Everglades by the 19th-century US-Seminole Wars—are acknowledged with numerous everyday items. Evocative photographs capture the Miami and Coconut Grove of the 1890s and the meeting of the 350 residents that formed Miami into a city in 1896. The museum also documents the arrival of the railroad, the 1920s land boom and the growth of tourism.

Miami Art Museum The art museum has well-designed galleries with excellent and diverse exhibitions of modern and contemporary art from around the world, focusing on work post-1945.

THE BASICS

🔁 E3
✉ 101 W Flagler Street
🚇 Government Center
🚌 All serving Downtown

Historical Museum
☎ 305/375-1492
🕐 Mon–Wed, Fri, Sat
10–5, Thu 10–9, Sun 12–5
♿ Good 💲 Inexpensive

Miami Art Museum
☎ 305/375-3000
🕐 Tue–Fri 10–5;
3rd Thu of month 10–9;
Sat, Sun 12–5
♿ Good 💲 Inexpensive

Miami Children's Museum

Attractions include the Mt. MiChiMu climbing wall, a bank and the "Sea and Me" gallery

THE BASICS

www.miamichildrens
museum.org

➕ G2

✉ 980 MacArthur
Causeway (I-395),
Watson Island

☎ 305/373-5437

🕐 Daily 10–6

🍴 Café

🚇 C, K, F/M, S

💲 Expensive

♿ Good

HIGHLIGHTS

● Dressing up
● Museum of Art
● Loading freight onto a
boat by remote crane
● Teddy Bear Museum
● Mt. MiChiMu climbing wall

From a breezy site overlooking the bay on the causeway out to Miami Beach, this well-thought-out family museum offers hours of hands-on fun for the young and young-at-heart.

MiChiMu The eye-catching exterior design of MiChiMu (as it likes to be known) originated on the drawing boards of Miami's home-grown celebrity architects Arquitectonia. It sets the tone for an equally quirky and imaginative interior lay-out, starting with the giant light-filled cone of the entrance hall. There are 14 galleries to explore and over 25,000sq ft (2,300sq m) of exhibition space packed with interactive exhibits, many of them crafted by those clever folks who help put the magic into Disney and Universal in Orlando. If the kids are into role-playing, they can weigh their own lobsters in the supermarket, man the Fire Station and play doctors and nurses. If there's energy to burn, head for the outdoor play area designed by local Miccousukee Indians, or tackle Mt. MiChiMu, the museum's 32ft (10m) rock-climbing wall.

Art Attack For the more sophisticated young person, there is a television studio where you can put together a weather report and see yourself on the small screen; a karaoke suite; and the opportunity to conduct a band. The Teddy Bear Museum is cute and perennially popular, and the Museum of Art both educates and invites budding artists to create their own masterpieces to adorn the walls.

See parrots galore, whether it's models at the entrance or the real thing inside

Parrot Jungle Island

Parrot shows and animal encounters, flower gardens and flamingo ponds are all part of the charm of this compact zoological attraction, easily reached from Downtown and Miami Beach.

Flower power Parrot Jungle, one of Miami's longest-running attractions, moved to Biscayne Bay from its former base to the south of the city in 2003. Famed for its lush gardens, the new "jungle" still has a little way to go before its grounds are as impressive as the old one, but the Everglades Habitat is looking good and is well-stocked with traditional Floridian wildlife, the flamingos are in the pink and the parrots are as chatty as ever.

Showtime If you've never seen a performing parrot, prepare to be amazed. Parrot Jungle's Winged Wonders show is quite a spectacle and features not only talkative parrots and talented macaws up to all kinds of tricks and stunts, but also swooping condors and Mama Cass, the Australian cassowary, 6ft (1.8m) tall. Big cats are the main attraction at Wild Encounters, another popular show, which combines a conservation message with fluffy baby tigers and the rare and handsome part-lion, part-tiger liger. Meet the spider monkeys at the Manú Encounter, while pythons, 20ft (6m long), hooded cobras and a spooky albino alligator keep audiences on the edge of their seats at the Serpentarium. In between shows, there are giant tortoises and an aviary to visit, and little kids can enjoy the Petting Barn.

THE BASICS

www.parrotjungle.com

➕ G2

✉ 111 Parrot Jungle Trail, MacArthur Causeway (I-395), Watson Island

☎ 305/400-7000

🕐 Daily 9.30–6

🍴 Café

🚌 C, K, F/M, S

♿ Few

💲 Expensive

HIGHLIGHTS

● Everglades Habitat Walk
● Feeding the parrots
● Reptile Giants show
● Winged Wonders show

More to See

ALFRED I DUPONT BUILDING
Completed in 1938, this handsome bank building is a fine example of the Depression-era Moderne style. In the lobby, admire the lavish art deco flourishes.
E3 169 E Flagler Street Miami Avenue All serving Downtown

BACARDI BUILDING
The Miami HQ of the Bacardi rum business is a MiMo (Miami Modern) icon from the 1960s. The blue-and-white tile-and-glass rectangle is perched on pedestals by Biscayne Boulevard in front of a second building featuring a glass mosaic created in France and shipped to Miami.
Off map at E1 2100 Biscayne Boulevard 305/573-8511 3, 16

BAYSIDE MARKETPLACE
On the bay, fronting the Downtown district, this is one of Miami's busiest attractions. There are more than 150 shops, stalls, restaurants and bars, and visitors are also entertained by street performers. The dockside bustles with charter-boat and boat-tour operators (▷ below). Music enhances the atmosphere at night and there are horse-and-carriage rides around the adjacent Bayfront Park, a green space dredged from the bay in the 1920s and now home to a 10,000-seat amphitheater used for concerts.
F3 401 N Biscayne Boulevard 305/577-3344 Mon–Thu 10–10, Fri–Sun 10am–11pm Bayfront Park 3, 16, 48, 95, C, S

BOAT TOURS
The Island Queen offers a leisurely, narrated harbor cruise past the Port of Miami and celebrity homes on Star Island, departing from Bayside Marketplace. If you are feeling more adventurous, take a kayak tour of Key Biscayne (▷ 84), rent a sailboat at Matheson Hammock Park (▷ 97) or visit the reef by glass-bottomed boat at Biscayne National Park (▷ 94–95).
F3 Island Queen, Bayside Marketplace, 401 Biscayne Boulevard 305/370-5119 or 800/910-5119 Daily Adequate Expensive

The Atlantis Apartments have a square hole through the middle

BRICKELL AVENUE AND THE ATLANTIS

One of Miami's early pioneers, William Brickell (rhymes with "nickel") ran an Indian trading post on the south bank of the Miami River and owned land extending from the river down to Coconut Grove. This was the city's original Millionaires' Row, lined with gracious homes, most of which have since been buried beneath modern concrete and glass monuments to the mighty dollar. Today, Brickell Avenue is Miami's towering Financial District, a glittering canyon of office buildings and condominiums, most of which are impressive without being architecturally distinguished. The one real gem is the Atlantis Apartments building, the 1983 *tour de force* of local architecture firm Arquitectonica, now rather dwarfed by its surroundings. The building's trademark quirk is a cutaway section, a square window five floors high through the middle of the building, furnished with a palm tree, a red-painted spiral staircase and a Jacuzzi for the use of residents, who can also work out at a gym housed in

the "missing" section located at ground level. Other notable Arquitectonica designs nearby include another condo, the Palace (1541 Brickell Avenue), and the bayfront American Airlines Arena.

➕ E4 **Atlantis Apartments** Off map at E5
✉ 2025 Brickell Avenue 🚗 Private residences; view from street only 🚇 5th Street/Financial District 🚌 24, 48, 95, B

CARNIVAL CENTER FOR THE PERFORMING ARTS

www.carnivalcenter.org

A symbol of Downtown rejuvenation, the stunning Carnival Center was designed by Argentinian Cesar Pelli and opened in 2006. The $500 million venue flanks Biscayne Boulevard and has an opera-house-cum-theater, studio theater, 2,200-seat concert hall and enormous plaza. The 1929 art deco Sears Tower is preserved from the old department store that once stood on the site.

➕ E2 ✉ 1300 Biscayne Boulevard
☎ 786/468-2000 🍴 Café/restaurant
🚇 Omni Station 🚌 3, 16, 93, 95, K, M
♿ Good

Palm trees frame the entrance to Hooters restaurant at Bayside Marketplace

The Freedom Tower (▷ 34) was once a processing center for Cuban refugees

DADE COUNTY COURTHOUSE

The classically inspired 27-floor Dade County Courthouse dates from 1926, when it was the tallest building in Florida. It culminates in a ziggurat peak. ✚ E3 ✉ 73 W Flagler Street ☺ Miami Avenue ☺ All serving Downtown

FREEDOM TOWER

Completed in 1925, the Freedom Tower was based on the Giralda bell tower of Seville Cathedral in Spain. It originally housed newspaper offices, but stood empty for several years until the US government co-opted it as a processing venue for Cuban refugees in 1962. Almost 300,000 Cubans arrived in Miami on the "freedom flights" from Havana that continued until 1974. Many received assistance and even lodgings in the building. Since then the handsome, but rather impractical, tower has remained closed despite a $25-million renovation in the 1980s. ✚ E3 ✉ 600 Biscayne Boulevard ☺ View from street only ☺ Freedom Tower ☺ 3, 16, 48, 95, C, S

GESÚ CHURCH

Serving Miami's oldest Catholic parish, established in 1896, the 1920s Gesú Church is richly decorated inside. Services are in English or Spanish. ✚ E3 ✉ 118 NE 2nd Street ☺ 1st Street ☺ Most serving Downtown

INTERNATIONAL PLAZA

The focal point of International Plaza is I M Pei's 48-floor Bank of America Tower, known for its nighttime illuminations. The ingenious late-1980s design appears to be a cut-away cylinder. ✚ E4 ✉ 100 SE 2nd Street ☺ Knight Center ☺ All serving Downtown

LITTLE HAITI

A bit of a rough diamond, this lively district north of Downtown has a Caribbean buzz. The Caribbean Marketplace (5925 NE 2nd Avenue), a copy of the famous *marché* in Port-au-Prince, is designated for restoration and there are also Creole restaurants. ✚ Off map at E1 ✉ NE 2nd Avenue, from 40th to 85th streets 🍴 Cafés/restaurants ☺ 9, 10

The eye-catching roof of Little Haiti's Caribbean Marketplace

The Metromover, dwarfed by one of Downtown's skyscrapers

Around Downtown

This gentle stroll around the historic Downtown district takes in cultural and architectural highlights.

DISTANCE: 1.5 miles (2.5km) **ALLOW:** 1.5 hours

START

BISCAYNE BOULEVARD at SE 1st Street
✚ F4 🅜 Bayside Station 🚌 3, 16, C, S

1 Start from Biscayne Boulevard and walk east on SE 1st Street, with a good view of International Plaza's Bank of America Building (▷ 34) up ahead to the left.

2 Turn right onto SE 2nd Avenue. Opposite the elaborate facade of the Gusman Center for the Performing Arts (▷ 38), take a quick look into the Ingraham Building (25 SE 2nd Avenue). Photographs in the lobby show the building under construction during the autumn/winter of 1926–27.

3 At the next junction, with the elegant Alfred I DuPont Building (▷ 32) on the opposite corner, turn left onto W Flagler Street. A hotchpotch of architectural styles, shops and malls provide plenty to look at before reaching the Dade County Courthouse (▷ 34).

END

BISCAYNE BOULEVARD at NE 2nd Street
✚ F3 🅜 Bayside Station 🚌 3, 16, C, S

7 From the church, turn right (east) on NE 2nd Street, which will lead you back to Biscayne Boulevard. Across the boulevard, you can see Bayside Marketplace (▷ 32) and the green expanse of Bayfront Park.

6 At NE 1st Avenue, turn left (north) for the pink-and-white wedding-cake structure of Gesú Church (▷ 34) on the corner of NE 2nd Street.

5 Head back to street level and walk north along 1st Avenue, with the Metromover tracks overhead for one block, then cross the street carefully and walk east on NW 1st Street between the modern courthouse buildings. This is the Jewelry District.

4 Across W 1st Avenue, climb the steps up to the Miami-Dade Cultural Center (▷ 28–29), laid out around a Mediterranean-inspired piazza. This is a good place for a drink.

Shopping

BAYSIDE MARKETPLACE
See page 32.

LA CASA DE LAS GUAYABERAS
Comfortable and ideally suited to warm climes, the billowing Cuban shirts known as *guayaberas*, so loved by elderly Cuban men strolling Little Havana, also make a sensible purchase for visitors to wear around town and take home as a souvenir. Buy off the peg or made to measure.
✚ Off map ✉ 5840 SW 8th Street ☎ 305/266-9683 🚌 8

EL CRÉDITO CIGAR FACTORY
Watch the experts (many of them Cuban expats) hand-rolling cigars the old-fashioned way before you buy.
✚ Off map ✉ 1106 SW 8th Street, Little Havana ☎ 305/858-4162 🚌 8, 12, 17, 208

GALERIA INTERNACIONAL MALL
This effervescent Downtown mall draws mainly Latin American tourists, mostly seeking clothing and electrical goods unavailable at home—or much cheaper.
✚ E3 ✉ 255 Flagler Street ☎ 305/371-4536 🚇 Miami Avenue 🚌 Any serving Downtown

HAITIAN ART FACTORY
If you enjoy Caribbean art, this gallery is well worth a visit. Art works include exotic landscapes and island portraits, woodcarvings, sculpture and pottery.
✚ Off map ✉ 835 NE 79th Street, Little Haiti ☎ 305/758-6939 🚌 2, 9, 10

HAVELI
Amid the sleek and painfully chic Design District showrooms, Haveli is a tiny oasis of tactile textiles, Oriental ceramics, Asian woodcarvings and funky Mexican mirrors.
✚ Off map ✉ 1376 NE 40th Street, Design District ☎ 305/573-0308 🚌 3, 9, 10, 16

HOLLY HUNT
A spectacular Design District showroom laid out over two floors, featuring top-of-the-range contemporary furnishings from the likes of Rose Tarlow and Christian Liaigre, as well as the Chicago-based designer's own-name collections.
✚ Off map ✉ 3833 NE 2nd Avenue ☎ 305/571-2012 🚌 9, 10

LUMINAIRE LAB
This is the crucible of the Kassamali brothers' highly regarded design empire, which has grown from a Miami lighting store founded in 1974. The sleek and impressive 7,500sq ft (695sq m) Lab has new and exclusive furniture, fittings and accessories for the home and office from top international manufacturers.
✚ Off map ✉ 3901 NE 2nd Avenue ☎ 305/575-5788 🚌 9, 10

MARUCHI CLOTHING OUTLET
Stylish threads from top designers, mostly for women, often at half their normal retail price.
✚ Off map ✉ 7861 SW 40th Street ☎ 305/266-7136 🚌 40

SEYBOLD BUILDING
Originally a bakery, this 10-floor 1920s building now houses almost 300 jewelry vendors. You can have lunch here too, and an armored car service will take significant purchases back to your hotel.
✚ E3 ✉ 36 NE 1st Street ☎ 305/374-7922 🚇 Miami Avenue 🚌 Any serving Downtown

---

SMOKER'S CHOICE

Cuba's tobacco industry and the many Cubans resident in Miami conspire to make the city one of the best places in the US to find fine cigars. Although importing genuine Cuban cigars is illegal, discerning smokers find much to please at the El Crédito Cigar Factory (▷ this page); La Tradicion Cubana (226 E Flagler Street); Stogie's (11612 SW 88th Street) and Cigar Connection (534 Lincoln Road Mall).

Entertainment and Nightlife

AMERICAN AIRLINES ARENA

Home to the NBA's Miami HEAT (Oct–Apr), this multipurpose waterfront auditorium, seating 20,000, stages major concerts and large-scale sports and arts events.
🚹 F2/3 ✉ 601 Biscayne Boulevard ☎ 786/777-1000 🚇 Freedom Tower 🚌 Any serving Bayside Marketplace

BAYSIDE MARKETPLACE

Enjoy free samba, salsa, reggae or rock during the afternoon at this open-air shopping mall (▷ 32).
🚹 F3 ✉ 401 Biscayne Boulevard ☎ 305/577-3344 🚇 College/Bayside 🚌 3, 16, 48, 95, C, S

CARNIVAL CENTER FOR THE PERFORMING ARTS

The Carnival Center (▷ 33) has four resident companies—the Florida Grand Opera, Miami City Ballet, Concert Association of Florida and the New World Symphony—and hosts visiting productions.
🚹 E2 ✉ 1300 Biscayne Boulevard ☎ 786/468-2000 🚇 Omni Station 🚌 3, 16, 93, 95, K, M ♿ Good

CHURCHILL'S HIDEAWAY

Poky and smoky, this is a popular venue for the best local indie rock, heavy metal, R&B and more.
🚹 Off map ✉ 5501 NE 2nd Avenue, Little Haiti ☎ 305/757-1807 🚌 9, 10

GUSMAN CENTER FOR THE PERFORMING ARTS

This sumptuous, beautifully restored 1920s theater hosts concerts, the Miami Film Festival and performances by many of the country's best mid-size performing arts troupes.
🚹 E3 ✉ 174 E Flagler Street ☎ 305/374-2444 🚇 Miami Avenue 🚌 Any serving Downtown

HOY COMO AYER

A sultry taste of old Havana, this intimate Calle Ocho cabaret is renowned for great music, Latino songs of love and loss, oodles of atmosphere and dancing until late.
🚹 A4 ✉ 2212 SW 8th Street, Little Havana ☎ 305/541-2631 🚌 8, 22, 208

MUSIC IN THE OPEN AIR

Barely a month passes without some kind of open-air concert in Miami. Major events include the Miami Reggae Festival (August at Bayfront Park) and the music-dominated Carnaval Miami, also known as Calle Ocho Festival (March in Little Havana). Or catch June's Goombay Festival in Coconut Grove's Peacock Park, Bayfront Park's Brazilian Festival in September and, at the same venue, November's Puerto Rican Festival.

NOCTURNAL

A megaclub laid out over three floors and a terrace.
🚹 E2 ✉ 50 NE 11th Street, Park West ☎ 305/576-6996 🚇 11th Street 🚌 9, 10, K, T

SPACE

Not for the fainthearted, this monster dance club has an open-air roof terrace that could host a football game and a diet of pounding progressive house and hip-hop.
🚹 E2 ✉ 34 NE 11th Street, Park West ☎ 305/350-1956 🚇 11th Street 🚌 9, 10, K, T

SOHO LOUNGE

This hangout for a cool crowd attracts excellent international music acts. Indie rock, industrial, freestyle, hip-hop and house appear, plus a Saturday Goth party.
🚹 Off map ✉ 175 NE 36th Street, Design District ☎ 305/576-1988 🚌 3, 9, 10, 16

STUDIO A

On the 11th Street club corridor, but definitely not part of it, this mid-size venue is one to watch if you're into live indie rock.
🚹 E2 ✉ 60 NE 11th Street, Park West ☎ 305/358-7625 🚇 11th Street 🚌 9, 10, K, T

TOBACCO ROAD

Tobacco Road is Miami's oldest bar and its most atmospheric setting for top blues and jazz artists.
🚹 E4 ✉ 626 S Miami Avenue ☎ 305/374-1198 🚇 5th Street 🚌 6, 8, 24, 48, 95, B

Restaurants

PRICES

Prices are approximate, based on a three-course meal for one person.

$$$	over $40
$$	$20–$40
$	under $20

AZUL ($$$)

This elegant, polished gastronomic establishment offers fine bay views through floor-to-ceiling windows. It serves delicate, artfully presented nouvelle cuisine, from the appetizer-size trio of tuna to aged Kobe beef and ethereal vanilla souffle for dessert.
✚ F5 ✉ Mandarin Oriental Hotel, 500 Brickell Key Drive
☎ 305/913-8358 🚌 248

BIG FISH ($$–$$$)

Enjoy top-notch seafood in a deceptively rustic setting beside the Miami River, with views of the passing cargo boats.
✚ E4 ✉ 55 SW Miami Avenue Road ☎ 305/373-1770 Ⓜ Riverwalk
🚌 6, 8

BONGO'S CUBAN CAFÉ ($$–$$$)

This huge Cuban-theme restaurant and nightclub on the bayfront is owned by Miami Sound Machine diva Gloria Estefan. Perch on a bongo-shape bar stool for a *mojito*, dine on chicken and rice or roast pork and plantains, and then salsa the night away.

✚ F3 ✉ 601 Biscayne Boulevard ☎ 786/777-2100
Ⓜ Freedom Tower 🚌 3, 16, 93, 95 C, S

LA CARRETA ($)

You can't miss the signature wagon wheel perched outside this Cuban classic. La Carreta opens 24 hours a day and serves good-value fillers like the lightly

MIAMI MENU READER

Adobo: Cuban marinade of sour orange juice, garlic, cumin and oregano.

Batido: Hispanic milk shake of fruit, ice and sweetened condensed milk.

Boliche: Cuban pot roast.

Chimichurri: Sauce made from parsley, garlic and olive oil, to go with...

Churrasco: Nicaraguan grilled marinated beef tenderloin.

Enchilado: Seafood in Cuban-style creole sauce.

Frijoles negros: Black beans.

Lechon asado: Roast suckling pig.

Mojito: Cuban cocktail of rum, lime, yerbabuena and soda water.

Mojo: Cuban sauce of garlic and sour orange juice.

Picadillo: Ground beef served with olives, capers and raisins.

Tamale: Cornmeal pastry cooked in a corn husk.

Yuca: Cassava root.

toasted *medianoche* (midnight sandwich) stuffed full of ham, roasted pork, Swiss cheese and pickles.
✚ Off map ✉ 3632 SW8 Street, Little Havana
☎ 305/444-7501 🚌 6, 8

CASA JUANCHO ($$$)

A long-time Miami favorite, this mock-castle has heavy wood tables, tiled floors and hearty food. You could be in Spain.
✚ Off map ✉ 2436 SW 8th Street, Little Havana
☎ 305/642-2452 🚌 8

FIDELE SEAFOOD ($)

Sample robust Haitian cooking at rock-bottom prices. Dishes include red snapper in tomato broth bursting with taste, Caribbean stews and BBQ ribs, all served with rice 'n' peas, vegetables and salad.
✚ Off map ✉ 7372 Biscayne Boulevard, Little Haiti ☎ 305/756-8886
🚌 9, 10

GARCIA'S SEAFOOD GRILLE ($)

This friendly, family-run riverside eatery has daily seafood specials supplied fresh from the fish market. The menu includes substantial chowders, stone crabs, conch salads and shrimp.
✚ D3 ✉ 398 NW North River Drive ☎ 305/375-0765
Ⓜ Government Center
🚌 Any serving Downtown

GRASS ($$$)

As its name suggests, Grass has a fern-fringed outdoor lounge and straw-thatched seating area with a stunning backlit bar decorated with flower-filled apothecary jars. The Asian-American menu features plenty of seafood; the Friday night BBQ is a magnet for hip Design District types, and there's music on weekends.

🚩 Off map ☒ 28 NE 40th Street, Design District
☎ 305/573-3355
🕔 Dinner Wed–Sat only
🚌 3, 9, 10, 16

GUAYACAN ($$)

Guayacan offers Nicaraguan eating at a reasonable cost. The menu is strongly meat-oriented, though there are several tempting seafood choices and great *sopas*.

🚩 A4 ☒ 1933 SW 8th Street
☎ 305/649-2015 🚌 8

LOMBARDI'S BAYSIDE MARKETPLACE ($$)

The Italian menu offers plenty of choice, from crusty *bruschetta* and thin-crust pizzas to more substantial trattoria-style fare. Round off the meal with a refreshing *gelato*. The outdoor tables are a great place to watch the world go by.

🚩 F3 ☒ 401 Biscayne Boulevard ☎ 305/381-9580
🕔 College/Bayside 🚌 3, 16, 95, C, S

LOS RANCHOS OF BAYSIDE ($$–$$$)

This popular Nicaraguan steak house serves top-notch beef with spicy salsas, *mariquitas* and ultrasweet desserts.

🚩 F3 ☒ Bayside Marketplace, 401 Biscayne Boulevard ☎ 305/375-8188
🕔 College/Bayside 🚌 3, 16, 48, 95, C, S

MICHAEL'S GENUINE FOOD AND DRINK ($$–$$$)

Chef/owner Michael Schwartz has another winner on his hands with this unpretentious (but rapidly expanding, due to

FAMILY FUN

Miami is full of restaurants that are family-friendly and a lot of fun as well. Youngsters enjoy themed restaurants such as Hard Rock Café (Bayside Marketplace) and Johnny Rockets (3036 Grand Avenue, Coconut Grove; 728 Ocean Drive, South Beach). Star-struck kids want to go to Bongo's Cuban Café (▷ 39), Gloria Estefan's eatery at the American Airlines Arena, Downtown, and the current top choice is Barton G's, The Restaurant (▷ 59) for theatrical serving ideas and wonderful desserts. For sheer nostalgia, you can't beat the landmark 11th Street Diner (1065 Washington Avenue), with its excellent burgers and ice creams.

popular demand) dining room. Superb, mostly locally sourced, ingredients are used to make dishes such as shrimp and chorizo pizza, curried *mahi* wraps, sumptuous slow-roasted pork, wood roasted steaks and the desserts... Unbelievable value, charming service.

🚩 Off map ☒ 130 NE 40th Street (Atlas Plaza), Design District ☎ 305/573-5550
🚌 3, 9, 10, 16

PERRICONE'S MARKETPLACE AND CAFÉ ($–$$)

Gather the ingredients for a mouthwatering Mediterranean feast at this terrific Italian market in the Brickell area, or find a shady café table where you can enjoy tasty antipasti and pasta dishes.

🚩 E5 ☒ 15 SE 10th Street
☎ 305/374-9449 🕔 10th Street/Promenade Station
🚌 13, 24, 48, 95

VERSAILLES ($$$)

The chandelier-lit dining room sees endless dressed-up Cuban birthday and wedding functions. It's loud, and just watching as waiters bear trayfuls of tasty and absurdly inexpensive Cuban food through the packed tables is great fun.

🚩 Off map ☒ 3555 SW 8th Street, Little Havana
☎ 305/444-0240 🚌 8

Glamorous Miami Beach is the backdrop of countless fashion shoots and an oceanfront playground for the rich and famous. Its focus is the art deco district, South Beach (or SoBe), where you'll find much of the city's finest shopping, dining and clubbing.

Fontainebleau Hotel,
MiMo Districts,
*North Shore Open
Space Park*

DRIVE
Flamingo drive
Flamingo Place
Lake
Pancoast
24th St.
City
Creek
Traymore
Roney
Palace
Boardwalk
23rd Street
COLLINS
AVENUE
Miami Beach Drive
Holiday Inn –
South Beach
Miami Beach
Cultural Campus
St
Miami Beach
Library
Beach
Collins
Park
Days Inn
The Setai
Shore Club
Riande
Shelborne
Raleigh
Richmond
South Seas
Marseilles
Surfcomber
Delano
The National
Sagamore
coln
ad
Ritz-
Carlton

Loews

Crowne Plaza
Royal Palm

Regent
South Beach
Ross
Grand Vacations
ven

ummus
ark

Patrol Station

eco Welcome Center
Front Auditorium

0   300 m
0   300 yds

South Beach
Fishing Pier

L   M   N

Bass Museum of Art

HIGHLIGHTS

● *The Tournament*, Flemish School
● *Crucifixion Triptych*, Van Haarlem

TIP

● The Bass has a busy calendar of gallery events and many of them are free with gallery admission. Check the website for details.

One of the area's earliest art deco buildings, this museum holds a priceless collection of paintings, sculpture and tapestries by European masters.

Architecture Fronted by gardens laid out in the 1920s, the Bass Museum of Art began life as a library that, in 1930, became the first public building in Miami designed with space for fine art exhibits. The architect gave Mayan features to the sturdy-looking structure of keystone, a type of coral rock from the Florida Keys, and had the main entrance decorated by bas-reliefs and wrought-iron sidelights. In the 1960s, the library became the Bass Museum of Art and the multimillion-dollar art collection of John and Johanna Bass was donated. In 2002, renowned architect Arata Isozaki's boxlike extension added further

Artworks on display include The Coronation of the Virgin with Saints *(c.1492) by Sandro Botticelli and Domenico Ghirlandaio (left) and Rubens'* The Flight of Lot and his Family from Sodom *(bottom, middle)*

much-needed exhibition space, enabling the museum to host visiting contemporary exhibitions.

Art The Basses had amassed some 500 European pieces, among them 167 paintings by artists as diverse as Peter Paul Rubens and Sir Thomas Lawrence, important 16th- and 17th-century textiles, and sculpture from the 15th to the 17th centuries. These items form the core of the museum's permanent collection: Cornelis van Haarlem's *Crucifixion Triptych* and Ferdinand Bol's *Venus and Adonis* are particularly impressive. Altogether grander, however, are a pair of immense 19th-century French-Belgian tapestries, *The Start of the Hunt* and *The Return from the Hunt*. Displayed nearby, *The Tournament*, of the 16th-century Flemish School, is among the most important tapestries on view in the United States.

THE BASICS

www.bassmuseum.org

➕ K1

✉ 2121 Park Avenue

☎ 305/673-7530

🕐 Tue–Sat 10–5, Sun 11–5

🚌 C, M, G, H, L, S, South Beach Local

♿ Good

🎨 Moderate

Holocaust Memorial

Heart-wrenching images at the Holocaust Memorial

THE BASICS

www.holocaustmmb.org

⊞ K2

✉ 1933–45 Meridian Avenue

☎ 305/538-1663

🕐 Daily 9–9

🚍 A, G, K, L, M, S, South Beach Local

♿ Good

🎟 Free

HIGHLIGHTS

● The Sculpture of Love and Anguish—the reaching arm
● The Lonely Path

Miami has one of the world's largest populations of Holocaust survivors. So it is fitting that a major memorial to the six million victims of Nazi genocide should stand here.

Lonely Path Visitors pass first through the Arbor of History, which outlines the story of the Jewish presence in Europe and the rise of Nazism. Horrifying photographs recall 1938's *Kristallnacht* and the cattle cars into which victims were packed for the journey to concentration camps. By far the most affecting section of the memorial is reached through the short tunnel named the Lonely Path, lined with the names of the most infamous concentration camps—the somber tunnel gradually diminishes in size to suggest the camps' role in diminishing the individual. Beyond the tunnel, you are confronted by Kenneth Treister's 42ft-high (13m) bronze statue of an arm and hand—visible from the street and reaching in anguish for the sky —and by nearly 100 tormented human figures.

Time for reflection Many of the sculptured figures are seeking to climb the raised arm to an open hand, representing freedom; some are scattered around the foreground. You have no choice but to walk among them—and when you do, you are crowded by indescribable suffering. The final section of the memorial holds the Memorial Wall, etched with thousands of Holocaust victims' names. The Reflective Pool, filled with oversized lilies, is a tranquil epilogue to the heart-wrenching story of atrocities and genocide.

Lincoln Road has boutiques, cafés, restaurants and theaters

Lincoln Road Mall

Once renowned as "the Fifth Avenue of the South," Lincoln Road is without doubt the most appealing shopping street in Miami. You don't even need to spend a fortune to enjoy its relaxed ambience.

Heyday Lincoln Road is Miami Beach in microcosm. Among the boutique windows, design emporiums, fine restaurants and cafés, you'll find architectural mementoes from its first great heyday in the 1920s and '30s. Notable landmarks include the Spanish Mission-style church (corner of Drexel Avenue) built in 1921 on land donated by developer Carl Fisher; the stylish tropical-deco Lincoln Theater (No. 555); handsome 1934 Mediterranean revival/art deco Colony Theater (No. 1040); and the superb Streamline Moderne Sterling Building (No. 927), with a glass block strip dramatically illuminated in blue after dark.

Rediscovered When Miami Beach was "rediscovered" by the Hollywood set in the 1950s, Morris Lapidus, architect of the Fontainebleau Hotel and "father of MiMo" (Miami Modern architecture), decreed that Lincoln Road should be pedestrian-only. It was a revolutionary concept at the time, but it worked and visitors are still enjoying his landscaped oasis of shady trees and water features that invites shoppers to slow down to a gentle stroll and take time out for a drink and a spot of people-watching. One of the nicest times to visit Lincoln Road is at sunset, when you can sit at a café table and watch the scenery shift from day to night as the lights come on.

THE BASICS

🔲 K2
✉ Lincoln Road Mall
🍴 Cafés/restaurants
🚌 C, G, H, K, L, M, S, South Beach Local

HIGHLIGHTS

● People-watching from the Café at Books & Books (▷ 59)
● Britto Central (▷ 55)
● Jonathan Adler's showroom (▷ 56)
● The Sterling Building

TIP

● It's always interesting—and often instructive—to drop in at ArtCenter/South Florida (✉ 800, 810 and 924 Lincoln Road ☎ 305/674-8278). This artists' collective, founded in 1984, houses galleries, classrooms and some 52 studios where you can view upcoming artists at work.

South Beach

South Beach, or SoBe, is the local soubriquet for Miami Beach's celebrated art deco district, a 12-block neighborhood that packs more than 1,200 architectural gems into an area bounded by 5th Street and 23rd Street.

The jet set SoBe is a magnet for sun lovers and party people, clubbers, hipsters, fashionistas, gays, straights and the just plain curious. Rocketed to international fame courtesy of an ephemeral 1980s TV show, *Miami Vice*, as well as by fashion photographers bewitched by the fabulous backdrop and light, South Beach became one of the most recognizable jet-set haunts of the late 20th century. Its earliest art deco buildings, dating from the mid-1920s, are richly decorated with local images such as palm trees and flamingos in a

Take a stroll down Ocean Drive, with its art deco buildings, or relax on the beach

style known as "tropical deco." The less whimsical Moderne style from the late-1930s celebrated a new age of streamlined aerodynamic designs, along with new materials such as chrome, glass block and neon.

South Beach today SoBe's main drag is Ocean Drive, where striking art deco hotels face the Atlantic across the green swathe of Lummus Park. Restaurants and cafés squeezed up against the sidewalk invite you to sit back and admire the endlessly fascinating parade of pedestrians, dog walkers, skaters and limos that regularly brings the traffic to a standstill during the long neon-lit evenings. Later on, the action moves to the clubs on Washington Avenue until, all too soon, dawn brings back that magical light so prized by photographers.

THE BASICS

🚩 K3
✉ The area bounded by 5th Street and 23rd Street
🍴 Cafés/restaurants
🚌 C, H, K, South Beach Local
ℹ Art Deco Welcome Center (Miami Design Preservation League), 1001 Ocean Drive, tel 305/531-3484
❓ Walking tours Wed–Sun (expensive; www.mdpl.org)

The Wolfsonian-FIU

The Wolfsonian building (left); Continuous Profile of Mussolini sculpture (middle); interior gallery (right)

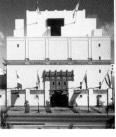

THE BASICS

www.wolfsonian.org

🔠 K4

✉ 1001 Washington Avenue

☎ 305/531-1001

🕐 Summer Mon, Tue, Sat, Sun 12–6, Thu, Fri 12–9; winter Thu, Fri 12–9, Sat, Sun 12–6

🚌 C, H, K, South Beach Local

🚻 Excellent

✋ Moderate; free Fri 6–9

HIGHLIGHTS

● Tours (Thu, Fri 6pm; Fri tour is free)
● Propaganda posters
● 19th-century cinema facade

You might see an Eiffel Tower-shape teapot, or maybe a machine for testing the chewing ability of the average mouth. Whatever you encounter at the hard-to-define Wolfsonian, it will be intriguing.

The background A member of a prominent Miami family, known for its entertainment and media empire, Mitchell Wolfson Jr is an avid collector with a special passion for art and design items of between 1885 and 1945. Confronted by high storage costs for his collection of more than 70,000 pieces, Wolfson simply bought a warehouse, a 1927 architectural landmark and the current site of the Wolfsonian. Refusing to be labeled a museum or institution, the Wolfsonian houses a design research center and public galleries, amid the art deco buildings of South Beach. The Wolfsonian's white facade is near-windowless so your attention is drawn to the intricate Spanish baroque bas-reliefs, which subtly pull you toward the entrance.

The exhibitions Many of the interior fittings are drawn from the collection, and none is more stunning than the green and gold terra-cotta facade of a 1920s Pennsylvania cinema that rises in the lobby. Inside, elevated walkways connect the galleries and give views across the South Beach rooftops. Exhibitions usually last several months and feature anything from Italian Futurist posters to Moderne cocktail shakers. Rather than simply presenting the objects or artworks, the exhibitions aim to highlight their cultural and technological context, making for stimulating viewing.

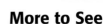

BOARDWALK

The Miami Beach Boardwalk runs between 21st and 46th streets, dividing the broad sandy beach from the sprawling ocean-view hotels and condominiums lining Collins Avenue. It can be reached from any of the adjoining streets, and with its shady resting places and walk-in access to several hotel cafés and bars, it's a popular spot for exercise, dog-walking, posing and people-watching, plus the views across the beach to the ocean are unbeatable.

➕ L1 ✉ Along the beach between 21st and 46th streets 🍴 Several hotel cafés and bars ♿ Good 💲 Free

CASA CASURINA

An Ocean Drive landmark for years, Casa Casurina achieved more recent notoriety as the spot where designer Gianni Versace was shot on his front steps in 1997. The magnificent 1930 Mediterranean Revival-style mansion is said to have been based on Diego Columbus' 16th-century palace in Santo Domingo. Today, its huge antique wooden doors bar the general public from what is now a private club.

➕ K3 ✉ 1114 Ocean Drive ◎ View from sidewalk only 🚌 C, H, K, South Beach Local

ESPAÑOLA WAY

Not a fan of the art deco architecture springing up along his "Fifth Avenue South" at Lincoln Road, Carl Fisher decided to create an alternative retail enclave in his preferred Mediterranean Revival style. The result was Española Way, a pretty, tree-shaded, two-block run of shops and sidewalk cafés with striped awnings and wrought-iron decoration.

➕ K3 ✉ Off Washington, between 14th and 15th Streets 🍴 Restaurants/cafés 🚌 C, H, K, South Beach Local

FONTAINEBLEAU HOTEL

www.fontainebleau.com

Opened in 1954, the Fontainebleau is one of the showpieces of the MiMo period (▷ 52). Architect Morris Lapidus' daring designs and luxurious interiors made it popular with visiting

Some jog, some walk, while others cycle along Miami's Boardwalk

The Fontainebleau Hotel

Hollywood celebrities, including Bob Hope, Judy Garland and Bing Crosby, who stayed and entertained on-site. Movie credits include scenes in *Tony Rome*, with Frank Sinatra, and *The Bell Boy*, with Jerry Lewis.

🚫 Off map at L1 ✉ 4441 Collins Avenue ☎ 305/538-2000 ⏰ Public areas always open ⏹ Restaurants/cafés 🚌 G, H, L, T, S ♿ Good

MIMO DISTRICTS

The latest architectural buzz-word to hit the Miami design lexicon, MiMo (Miami Modern) describes the futuristic Florida architecture of the 1950s and 60s. Its chief exponent on Miami Beach was Morris Lapidus, who created the trendsetting curved facade of the 1954 Fontainebleau (▷ 51), and superbly restored Eden Roc (4525 Collins Avenue). The twin poles of MiMo are Miami Beach's North Beach Resort Historic District (63rd to 71st streets) and the Biscayne Boulevard Historic District (50th to 77th streets) on the mainland.

🚫 Off map at L1

NORTH SHORE OPEN SPACE PARK

This is a good family beach park for a picnic and an opportunity to run around. There are barbeque grills, a grassy park with plenty of shade behind the dunes leading down to the shore, a beach lifeguard and nature trail. If you want to take to two wheels, there's also a cycle path.

🚫 Off map at L1 ✉ 7929 Atlantic Way (off Collins Avenue between 78th Street and 87th Terrace) ☎ 305/673-7720 ⏰ Dawn–dusk 🚌 G, H, L, S, T ♿ Good 🆓 Free

SOFI

Yet another local acronym, SoFi (or South of Fifth) denotes the area south of 5th Street running down to South Pointe Park. Surprisingly untouched by the development of the art deco district until recently, SoFi can now boast its own clutch of bijou hotels and fine restaurants.

🚫 K5 ✉ The area south of 5th Street running down to South Pointe Park ⏹ Restaurants/cafés 🚌 H, M, South Beach Local

The Smith and Wollensky Restaurant, in South Pointe Park

South Beach Stroll

Blue skies, palm trees, sea, sand and Ocean Drive, this stroll takes you through Miami's world-famous art deco district.

DISTANCE: 1.25 miles (2km) **ALLOW:** 1.5 hours

START

OCEAN DRIVE at 5th Street
🚏 K4 🚌 C, H, K, M, South Beach Local

END

LINCOLN ROAD MALL
🚏 K2 🚌 C, G, H, K, L, M, S, South Beach Local

1 Start at 5th Street, the southern boundary of the Miami Beach art deco district, and head north along the dazzling art deco hotel strip fronting Ocean Drive. A couple of highlights here are the Park Central Hotel (No. 640, ▷ 111), with a spectacular telescoping lobby; and the tropical-deco-style Colony Hotel (No. 736).

7 At Española Plaza, turn right (north) on Drexel Avenue for a shady route past lovingly restored art deco apartment blocks to the Lincoln Road Mall (▷ 47).

2 The 800 block is home to the famous News Café (▷ 56), a good spot for breakfast or a drink. Sit out at a side-walk table and admire the view across Lummus Park to the Atlantic horizon.

6 Cross the road to drop into the United States Post Office (No. 1300) for the lobby mural depicting an early encounter between Spanish conquistadors and Native Americans. A block later turn left into Española Way (▷ 51).

3 A few doors down, the chic Pelican Hotel (▷ 111) has been restored, and the Waldorf Towers' (▷ 111) fanciful neon beacon featuring a mermaidlike bather is illuminated in the evening.

4 Opposite the Art Deco Welcome Center (No. 1001, ▷ 55), turn west on 10th Street for two blocks to Washington Avenue. The tall, windowless cream building on the right is home to the Wolfsonian-FIU (▷ 50).

5 Turn right and walk north on Washington, past the 11th Street Diner (▷ 59), in a historic aluminum railroad car. On the west side of the street, the imposing Mediterranean Revival-style Old City Hall dates from the 1920s.

WALK

MIAMI BEACH

Shopping

ARMANI EXCHANGE
Local branch of the internationally renowned designer of quality, stylish men's and womenswear. Look for the glass-block facade, neon-lit at night.
🔂 K4 ✉ 760 Collins Avenue ☎ 305/531-5900 🚇 C, H, K, South Beach Local

ART DECO WELCOME CENTER
Stock up on art deco district souvenirs, from glossy coffee-table design tomes to fridge magnets. Art postcards, posters and limited-edition black-and-white photographs are a good buy and there are plenty of little kitschy items for presents.
🔂 K3 ✉ 1001 Ocean Drive ☎ 305/531-3484 🚇 C, H, K, South Beach Local

BAL HARBOUR SHOPS
Nestled amid the lush tropical vegetation of this landscaped mall are big-spenders' favorites such as Gucci, Prada and Vuitton, alongside Saks Fifth Avenue and Neiman Marcus.
🔂 Off map ✉ 9700 Collins Avenue, Miami Beach ☎ 305/866-0311 🚇 G, K, R, S, T

BARNEYS CO-OP
The wayward offspring of sleek and stylish Barneys New York, the Co-op features an exciting range of more cutting-edge, youth-oriented designers, including Amanda Uprichard, Citizens of Humanity and Aristocrat.
🔂 K4 ✉ 832 Collins Avenue ☎ 305/421-2010 🚇 C, H, K, South Beach Local

BASE
This one-stop lifestyle store for the effortlessly hip has must-have micro collections of music, magazines, art and style tomes, clothes, shoes and home accessories.
🔂 K2 ✉ 939 Lincoln Road ☎ 305/531-4982 🚇 C, G, H, K, L, M, S, South Beach Local

BEATNIX
Stand out from the crowd by donning a bright orange jumper, a dayglo T-shirt or any combination of the distinctive multicolored clothing creations that are sold here.
🔂 K3 ✉ 1149 Washington Avenue ☎ 305/532-8733 🚇 C, H, K, South Beach Local

BOOKS & BOOKS
A real neighborhood bookstore with loads of events and an excellent café (▷ 59), as well as a good range of reading material and a particularly broad selection of Florida titles, both factual and fictional.
🔂 K2 ✉ 933 Lincoln Road ☎ 305/532-3222 🚇 C, G, H, K, L, M, S, South Beach Local

BRITTO CENTRAL
Miami's very own adopted artist-in-residence, Romero Britto (born 1963 in Brazil), is known for his bold, bright Cubist Pop Art. His studio-cum-retail showcase sells original artworks, limited-edition prints and collectibles.
🔂 K2 ✉ 818 Lincoln Road ☎ 305/531-8821 🚇 C, G, H, K, L, M, S, South Beach Local

DESIGN LAB
Street-smart Kimikai T-shirts and "notice-me!" swimwear for rock chicks, plus there's some boy stuff, too.
🔂 K3 ✉ 445 Española Way ☎ 305/531-4075 🚇 C, H, K, South Beach Local

EUTOPIA
Anyone popping in to grab a book for the beach could well end up spending hours poring through the copiously filled shelves laden with books of all kinds. The shop is especially strong on fiction and Florida titles.
🔂 K2 ✉ 1626 Jefferson Avenue ☎ 305/532-8680 🚇 C, H, K, M, S, South Beach Local

ESSENTIAL SKATES
Passing yourself off as a local in South Beach is hard to do without a pair of in-line skates attached to your feet and the skills necessary to stay upright and moving. A wide range of skates, along with heelies, can be bought or rented at Fritz's Skate, Bike and Surf (✉ 730 Lincoln Road ☎ 305/532 1954).

FLY BOUTIQUE
It's well worth browsing here for new and used designer clothing—anything from business suits to club wear—at tempting prices; there's also a stash of wacky jewelry.
K2 · 650 Lincoln Road · 305/604-8508 · C, H, K, M, S, South Beach Local

THE FRAGRANCE SHOP
If you've never been able to find the right perfume for you, come here and make your own using the shop's bottles of undiluted oils.
K2 · 612 Lincoln Road · 305/535-0037 · C, H, K, M, S, South Beach Local

INTERMIX
This New York boutique has brought its youthful sass to SoBe. In addition to its own lines, the shop stocks clothes by today's hottest designers, from John Bartlett and Jimmy Choo to Malia Mills and Chloe.
K4 · 634 Collins Avenue · 305/531-5950 · C, H, K, South Beach Local

JONATHAN ADLER
A consistently fun and funky showroom for Adler's vibrant designs, "where lonely sofas meet perky cushions" according to the blurb. And those delectable needlepoint cushions are indeed perky, affordable and eminently packable!

K2 · 1024 Lincoln Road · 305/534-5600 · C, G, H, K, L, M, S, South Beach Local

LUNATIKA
Inventively designed lamps, such as the Sputnik chandelier, paper lanterns and other cutting-edge items for the home are sold here.
J3 · 1562 Alton Road · 305/534-8585 · S, South Beach Local

NEWS CAFÉ
A popular South Beach hangout that offers a modest selection of fiction with a stronger stock of US and international newspapers.
K4 · 800 Ocean Drive · 305/538-6397 · C, H, K, South Beach Local

POP
A delightful collection of mass-culture knickknacks, from vintage refrigerator magnets to 1960s TV show annuals.
K3 · 1151 Washington Avenue · 305/604-9604 · C, H, K, South Beach Local

PUBLIX SUPERMARKETS
Florida-based Publix supermarkets are known for their low prices. In the South Beach branch, check out the neon-lit early 1960s architecture and look for glamorous faces jostling for position in the checkout lines (· 1045 Dade Boulevard · 305/534-4621).

RECYCLED BLUES
Allow plenty of time to browse through this voluminous collection of vintage clothing. As you might expect from the name, there's a particular emphasis on denim.
K3 · 1507 Washington Avenue · 305/538-0656 · C, H, K, South Beach Local

SOUTH BEACH DIVE AND SURF
You'll find surfboards, wetsuits and everything else for the beach and breakers here, with products by many leading names.
K4 · 850 Washington Avenue · 305/673-5900 · C, H, K, South Beach Local

SOUTH BEACH STYLE
This store sells everything for the style-conscious South Beach home, from art deco sofas and dining tables to attractive stationery sets, candles and gift items.
K2 · 1674 Meridian Avenue · 305/538-8277 · C, H, K, South Beach Local

TOMAS MAIER
Buy into the luxury lifestyle as perfected by the former creative director of Bottega Veneta. Capsule collections of clothes, fabulous swimwear, fragrances and artworks are displayed in a cool, minimalist villa.
J2 · 1800 West Avenue · 305/531-8383 · M, S, South Beach Local

ABBEY BREWING COMPANY

A delightful bar with a good list of its own-brewed ales and other microbrews.

🔲 J2 ✉ 1115 16th Street ☎ 305/538-8110 🚌 M, S

ARTURO SANDOVAL JAZZ CLUB

The fabulously retro Deauville Beach Resort provides a stylish MiMo setting for nightly jazz acts. Quite pricey drinks and dinner, but this is a classy joint and standards are high.

🔲 Off map ✉ 6701 Collins Avenue, Mid-Beach ☎ 305/865-5775 🚌 G, H, J, L, S, T

BUCK 15

Above kitschy Miss Yip's Chinese restaurant, this relaxed lounge-gallery gathers around a tiny bar with a collection of funky sofas and armchairs. With Sino-Japanese artwork and collectibles around the walls and cool DJ music, it's a great place to hang out.

🔲 K2 ✉ 707 Lincoln Lane ☎ 305/538-3815 🚌 C, H, K, M, S, South Beach Local

CLEVELANDER

Rock and infectious Latin dance rhythms spill across Ocean Drive from the popular poolside bar at this art deco hotel facing the beach.

🔲 K4 ✉ 1020 Ocean Drive ☎ 786/276-1414 🚌 C, H, K, South Beach Local

COLONY THEATER

An art deco landmark originally built by Paramount Studios as a cinema in 1934. Restored and reopened in 1976, the Colony now makes an intimate setting for chamber music and other productions.

🔲 J2 ✉ 1040 Lincoln Road ☎ 305/674-1026 🚌 C, H, G, L, M, S, South Beach Local

GLASS @ THE FORGE

The Forge is one of Miami's most enduring celebrity haunts, a classic steak house with a serious wine cellar and now this cool white leather lounge for young hipsters with a taste for New York house music. A strange juxtaposition, but it works.

🔲 Off map ✉ 432 41st Street, Mid-Beach ☎ 305/604-9798 🚌 G, H, J, L, S, T

SOUTH BEACH CLUBS

Admission to South Beach nightclubs is often restricted to the kind of people the club owners want to see inside. If a club is popular among celebrities, door managers admit only the famous, fashionable or glamorously attired. Most, however, admit anybody dressed with sensitivity to the style of the club. Expect long lines on Friday and Saturday nights. Cover charges of up to $20 are often waived before 9pm.

JACKIE GLEASON THEATER FOR THE PERFORMING ARTS

Touring orchestras and opera companies appear, including the American Ballet Theater in January.

🔲 K2 ✉ 1700 Washington Avenue ☎ 305/673-7300 🚌 C, H, G, L, M, S, South Beach Local

JAZID

Jazz nightly, rock, reggae and funk, this eclectic little showcase offers it all. Live music downstairs; DJs above.

🔲 K3 ✉ 1342 Washington Avenue ☎ 305/673-9372 🚌 C, H, K, South Beach Local

LAUNDRY BAR

Blame the Levis ad for this bizarre concept. Take your dirty washing along, pop it in the full-service laundromat and strike up a conversation over a drink while your togs whirl around in the suds. DJ music, gay-friendly with drag cabaret Saturday nights.

🔲 K2 ✉ 721 N Lincoln Lane (Meridian Avenue) ☎ 305/531-7700 🚌 C, H, K, M, S, South Beach Local

LINCOLN THEATRE

The home of the New World Symphony Orchestra, the United States' premier training orchestra for young musicians, who perform from October to May.

🔲 K2 ✉ 541 Lincoln Road ☎ 305/673-3331 🚌 C, H, G, L, M, S, South Beach Local

MANGO'S TROPICAL CAFÉ

Abandon all pretense at cool, SoBe-like behavior and go with the flow of this exuberant Latino celebration of music, dance and *mojitos*.

🞧 K4 ✉ 900 Ocean Drive
☎ 305/673-4422 🚌 C, H, K, South Beach Local

MANSION

SoBe megadance club in a former art deco movie theater with sweeping staircases and chandeliers, which has also hosted boxing matches and bands. International DJs play house, hip-hop, R&B and more.

🞧 K3 ✉ 1235 Washington Avenue ☎ 305/531-5535
🚌 C, H, K, South Beach Local

MIAMI BEACH CINEMATHEQUE

Fronted by a gallery and bookstore, this little cinema, operated by the Miami Film Society, shows art-house movies in an intimate screening room.

🞧 K3 ✉ 512 Española Way
☎ 305/673-4567 🚌 C, H, K, South Beach Local

MYNT ULTRA LOUNGE

Dress for success to gain entry to this fashionable lounge-cum-dance club. The huge bar and squishy leather seating areas are bathed in another-worldly green light.

🞧 L2 ✉ 1921 Collins Avenue ☎ 305/532-0727
🚌 C, G, H, L, M, S

NORMAN'S TAVERN

Far enough north from SoBe to be relaxed, this hangout is a great place to eat and drink while watching the world go by.

🞧 Off map ✉ 6770 Collins Avenue ☎ 305/868-9248
🚌 G, H, J, L, S, T

OPIUM GARDEN/ PRIVÉ

Right down in the heel of SoFi, the enormous Opium Garden courtyard is an open-air dance club decorated with buddhas and Chinese lanterns. It shares premises with the exclusive Privé lounge upstairs (access through a back alley), where celebrities and local A-listers gather for some of Miami Beach's best hip-hop parties.

🞧 K5 ✉ 136 Collins Avenue
☎ 305/531-5535 🚌 H, M, South Beach Local

PURDY LOUNGE

Unpretentious, side-street cocktail bar with pool table, music and a relaxed vibe. Swots might enjoy the Sunday night Spelling Bee.

🞧 K2 ✉ 1811 Purdy Avenue (18th Street) ☎ 305/531-4622 🚌 C, G, H, L, M, S

ROSEBAR

Splash out on a cocktail and participate in some superb people-watching at the ultrachic lobby bar of the Delano (▷ 112). Sink into a designer sofa or wander out to the beach deck.

🞧 L2 ✉ 1685 Collins Avenue ☎ 305/672-2000
🚌 C, G, M, H, L, S

SKYBAR

This glamorous watering hole is one of the hottest spots in town. Enjoy a drink in one of the outdoor bars, people-watch from a comfortable seat, peek into the famous Red Room and see who's getting up to no good in the VIP-only areas.

🞧 L2 ✉ The Shore Club, 1901 Collins Avenue
☎ 305/695-3100 🚌 C, G, H, L, M, S

VAN DYKE CAFÉ

In an upstairs room of this busy café, the cream of local jazz musicians demonstrate their skills to an appreciative crowd.

🞧 K2 ✉ 846 Lincoln Road
☎ 305/534-3600
🚌 C, G, H, K, L, M, S, South Beach Local

Restaurants

PRICES

Prices are approximate, based on a three-course meal for one person.

$$$ over $40
$$ $20–$40
$ under $20

11TH STREET DINER ($–$$)

A 1948 silver railroad dining car that began life in Pennsylvania has come to rest on the corner of 11th and Washington. Classic American fare is served up 24/7 to a mixed crowd of locals and visitors. Popular with the gay contingent, too.

➕ K3 ✉ 1065 Washington Avenue ☎ 305/534-6373 🚌 C, H, K, South Beach Local

A FISH CALLED AVALON ($$–$$$)

Lobster, king prawn and crab legs all show up on a seafood menu here, including Florida favorites such as grilled mahimahi and blackened grouper.

➕ K4 ✉ Avalon Hotel, 700 Ocean Drive ☎ 305/532-1727 🕐 Dinner only 🚌 C, H, K, South Beach Local

BALANS ($$)

Flavors from the Caribbean, Asia and Mediterranean pepper the menu, which also includes standbys such as grilled steak and sea bass. Tables outside.

➕ J2 ✉ 1022 Lincoln Road ☎ 305/534-9191 🚌 C, H, K, M, S, South Beach Local

BARTON G'S, THE RESTAURANT ($$$)

Deep-frozen nitro cocktails, a delicate arrangement of foie gras, nuts and berries on a mini-croissant crowned with a twinkling Eiffel tower, 3ft (90cm) tall, and ice-cream mountains studded with sparklers: This is food as theater, but the gimmicky presentation doesn't interfere with fine ingredients sympathetically prepared.

➕ J3 ✉ 1427 West Avenue ☎ 305/672-8881 🕐 Dinner 🚌 M, S, South Beach Local

BIG PINK ($–$$)

Cheeseburgers, baby back ribs and creatively ethnic dishes like Mexican shrimp calzone and Thai pasta are just a few of the foods served with South Beach style and New York attitude.

GET YOUR OATS

Healthy eating can be tricky on vacation and food allergy sufferers will find Miami surprisingly unprepared for conditions like wheat and gluten intolerance. However, there is help at hand at the Wild Oats Marketplace (✉ 1020 Alton Road ☎ 305/532-1707 🕐 Daily 7am–midnight), which offers fantastic picnic-makings from the deli counter, as well as fresh fruit, organic wines and a range of gluten-free and other special foods. There's a café, too.

➕ K5 ✉ 157 Collins Avenue ☎ 305/531-0888 🚌 H, M, South Beach Local

BLUE DOOR ($$$)

Creative, contemporary American cooking takes in tuna foie gras, open-faced ravioli served with rabbit, and Maine lobster in coconut milk broth.

➕ L2 ✉ Delano Hotel, 1685 Collins Avenue ☎ 305/674-6400 🚌 C, G, M, H, L, S

CAFÉ AT BOOKS & BOOKS ($–$$)

A peaceful oasis with window seats and sunny sidewalk tables for an espresso or a glass of wine to accompany a panini and a spot of people-watching. The evening menu features more elaborate South Florida-style entrées.

➕ K2 ✉ 933 Lincoln Road ☎ 305/695-8898 🚌 C, G, H, K, L, M, S, South Beach Local

CAFFÈ MILANO ($$)

North-Italian cooking in unpretentious surroundings.

➕ K4 ✉ 850 Ocean Drive ☎ 305/532-0707 🚌 C, H, K, W

CHEF ALLEN'S ($$$)

Allen Susser's artful cuisine is South Florida dining at its best. Enjoy dishes like bay scallops with sweet potato ravioli and red wine vinegar.

➕ Off map ✉ 19088 NE 29th Avenue (191st Street), North Miami Beach ☎ 305/935-2900 🕐 Dinner only

ESCOPAZZO ($$$)

A South Beach Italian-dining favorite, where the seafood and risottos are outstanding.

🚻 K3 ✉ 1311 Washington Avenue ☎ 305/674-9450 🚍 C, H, K, South Beach Local

FRATELLI LA BUFALA ($$)

Raising consciousness of things buffalo, the edible parts anyway, this is the place to sample real buffalo mozzarella, ricotta, steaks and the rest on fabulous thin-crust, Neapolitan-style pizzas.

🚻 K4 ✉ 437 Washington Avenue ☎ 305/532-0700 🚍 H, M, South Beach Local

JOE'S STONE CRAB ($$$)

You'll have to stand in line at this landmark to tuck into the stone crabs and mustard sauce, and perfect Key lime pie.

🚻 K5 ✉ 11 Washington Avenue ☎ 305/673-0365 🕐 Closed Aug, Sep 🚍 H, M, South Beach Local

LARIOS ON THE BEACH ($–$$)

Owned by Miami music stars Emilio and Gloria Estefan, this is a great place to sample new-style Cuban cuisine and live Cuban music.

🚻 K4 ✉ 820 Ocean Drive ☎ 305/532-9577 🚍 C, H, K, South Beach Local

NEMO ($$–$$$)

Innovative and seriously good American cuisine and fabulous desserts, in a trendy art deco building.

🚻 K5 ✉ 100 Collins Avenue ☎ 305/532-4550 🚍 H, M, South Beach Local

OLA AT THE SANCTUARY HOTEL ($$$)

Doug Rodriguez's light and innovative touch has realigned the general perception of South American cooking. *Ceviche*, plantain-crusted mahimahi and top-quality beef served by charming staff in a restful dining room.

🚻 K2 ✉ 1745 James Avenue ☎ 305/695-9125 🕐 Dinner only 🚍 C, G, H, L, M, S

OSTERIA DEL TEATRO ($$$)

It's elbow to elbow in Dino Pirola's tiny South Beach restaurant. Northern Italian cooking

---

TIME FOR BED

"Dinner in bed, dear?" Well, it makes a change from breakfast, so head for B.E.D. ($$$), where delicious dinners are served to a relaxed clientele lounging on, you've guessed it, beds. French-influenced cuisine includes a scrumptious pan-seared sea bass with a vermouth cream sauce and heavenly cappuccino crème brûlée (🚻 K4 ✉ 929 Washington Avenue ☎ 305/532-9070 🕐 Dinner only 🚍 C, H, K, South Beach Local).

---

gets no better than this. Beef is great, pasta exceptional (look for stone crab-filled ravioli in lobster sauce), desserts a must.

🚻 K3 ✉ 1443 Washington Avenue ☎ 305/538-7850 🚍 C, H, K, M, South Beach Local

PELICAN CAFÉ ($$)

Cameron Diaz, Antonio Banderas and Johnny Depp have all eaten in this industrial-chic Mediterranean café at the funkiest hotel in town.

🚻 K4 ✉ 826 Ocean Drive ☎ 305/673-3373 🚍 C, H, K, South Beach Local

PUERTO SAGUA ($)

Outliving most South Beach eateries, this old-time Cuban diner has a fabulous mural of Havana and stays open until 2am.

🚻 K4 ✉ 700 Collins Avenue ☎ 305/673-1115 🚍 C, H, K, South Beach Local

SANTO ($$$)

Urban cool restaurant with hip bar area, live music lounge and a modern American menu with Mediterranean/Asian accents.

🚻 K2 ✉ 420 Lincoln Road ☎ 305/532-2882 🕐 Dinner only 🚍 C, G, H, K, L, M, S, South Beach Local

VAN DYKE CAFÉ ($)

Popular for people-watching, with burgers, eggs Benedict and sandwiches.

🚻 K2 ✉ 846 Lincoln Road ☎ 305/534-3600 🚍 C, G, H, K, L, M, S, South Beach Local

Lush, lovely Coral Gables is Miami's original "City Beautiful." Elegant Mediterranean-style homes stand in curving, tree-lined streets, and there are manicured golf courses and grand hotels, plus some of the city's finest upscale shopping and dining.

Place
St Michel

Alhambra Street Circle

Giralda Avenue

Aragon Avenue Coral Gables Omni
Museum Colonnade

CORAL WAY MIRACLE MILE

† † Colonnade
City Building
Way Hall

Andalusia Avenue

Avenue Valencia Avenue

Almeria Avenue
Avenue

Seville Avenue
Sevilla Avenue

nue Palermo Avenue

atalonia Segovia Avenue Catalonia Avenue

alaga Avenue District
Court

Santander Avenue
Santander Avenue

Avenue San Sebastian Avenue

University Romano Avenue
Park
venue Sarto Avenue

venue Camilo Avenue

Aledo Avenue
Cadima Avenue
Coral Gables
Drive Cadima Avenue Trolley
French
Normandy Alesio Avenue
Village
Viscaya Avenue

Fluvia Avenue

Candia Avenue

Velarde Avenue

)TH STREET New BIRD AVENUE
Theatre

San Antonio Avenue

ltara Avenue
Italian
Village
San Lorenzo Avenue

teban Avenue Village of
Merrick Park
Jeronimo Drive

ORAL Vilabella Avenue
ABLES Alminar Avenue Greco Avenue

Cadagua Avenue

Florida Avenue

Grand Avenue

PONCE DE LEON BOULEVARD
SOUTH DIXIE HIGHWAY

Grant Drive

1

Loquat Avenue
Kunquat Avenue

Chinese Sansovino Avenue
Village Lybyer Avenue
Castania Avenue

Bianca Avenue

Perguia Avenue COCONUT
GROVE

0 250 m

0 250 yds

B C

Coral Gables

The Biltmore Hotel

The Biltmore's striking tower is based on Seville's baroque Giralda bell tower

THE BASICS

www.biltmorehotel.com

A7

✉ 1200 Anastasia Avenue Coral Gables

☎ 305/445-1926

🕐 Public areas always open; best to visit during daylight hours

🍴 Café and restaurant

🚌 152

♿ Good

💲 Free

❓ Free guided tours Sun at 1.30, 2.30, 3.30

HIGHLIGHTS

● Lobby with hand-painted ceiling
● Grand pool
● Terrace
● Everglades Suite (Al Capone Suite)

Few buildings better encapsulate the glamor of 1920s Miami than the Biltmore Hotel. Created at the height of the property boom, it was a popular winter-season destination for the rich and famous during that golden era.

Opulent openings Touted as "the last word in the evolution of civilization, the acme of hostelries and clubs," the Biltmore opened in 1926 to pamper a trainload of celebrities from New York. Boasting Italian marble, 8ft-high (2.5m) crystal chandeliers and an 18-hole golf course, the hotel was created by the architectural firm of Schultze & Weaver, later renowned for New York's Waldorf-Astoria Hotel. Biltmore guests were kept amused by tennis, fox-hunting, horseback-riding and fashion shows, and fed on pheasant and trout. They could dip in the mammoth-size pool under the eye of swimming instructor Johnny Weissmuller, future Olympic champion and Hollywood's most popular Tarzan.

Biltmore today The Depression ended the Biltmore's days of luxury, but in the 1980s the hotel was expensively restored, reopening in 1993. The elegance begins as you enter the lobby, topped by a vaulted ceiling and marked at one end by an enormous fireplace and leering gargoyles. Outside, stand on the exquisitely tiled terrace loggia and gaze out across the golf course and the pool. The hotel's 26-floor tower, based on Seville's baroque Giralda bell tower, is home to the most expensive guest rooms.

International Villages

George Merrick, creator of Coral Gables, was a promotional wizard, thinking up novel ideas to ensure his "City Beautiful" was never out of the news. One typically inventive plan was for a series of eye-catching International Villages.

Quirky Though Spanish/Mediterranean Revival was the original architectural remit for Coral Gables, Merrick later planned to build 14 quirky "villages" in architectural styles that spanned the globe. Work started on seven of these enclaves, which occupy only a couple of blocks each at most, but the property crash at the end of the 1920s bankrupted Merrick, and only half the villages were completed.

Treasure hunt Finding the villages is like a treasure hunt. The most striking example of Merrick's whimsical streak is the Chinese Village (off Riviera Drive at Menendez Avenue), with its pagoda roofs, bright paintwork and faux bamboo window grilles. At the other end of Riviera, the twisted barley-sugar chimney pots of a Dutch Colonial home are silhouetted against the blue Florida sky, and on Hardee Road the French Country (500 block) and French City (1,000 block) homes were based on northern French chateaux and elegant 18th-century town houses respectively. The best of the Italian Village houses (Altara at Palmarito Avenue) has a conical tower, fancy ironwork and tiles, while the Pioneer homes (Santa Maria Street) are reminiscent of the Greek Revival period. The French Normandy quarter (400 block of Viscaya, off LeJeune Road/SW 42nd Avenue) looks as pretty as a picture.

THE BASICS

Chinese Village ✚ B8/9
Dutch Colonial Village
✚ Off map
French City Village
✚ Off map
French Country Village
✚ Off map
French Normandy Village
✚ B7
Italian Village ✚ B8
Pioneer Village ✚ A8
◷ Best viewed during daylight hours
🛈 Information and local maps from the Coral Gables Chamber of Commerce, 224 Catalonia Avenue, tel 305/446-1657; Mon–Thu 9.30–5, Fri 9.30–4

HIGHLIGHTS

- Chinese Village
- Dutch Colonial Village
- French Normandy Village

Lowe Art Museum

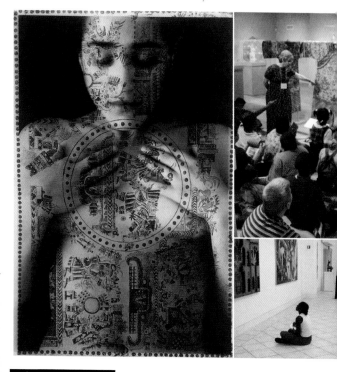

HIGHLIGHTS

● Anasazi effigy vessel
● *Madonna and Child Enthroned With Donors and Saints Dominic and Elizabeth of Hungary*, Lippo Vanni
● Lakota woman's dress
● *College Football Player*, Duane Hanson

TIP

● The Lowe doesn't have a café, but the nearby Titanic Brewery and Restaurant (▷ 73) serves good food and home-brewed beers.

The Lowe Art Museum has long held an extensive collection of European art. It has more recently acquired a reputation for its Native American collections, as well as the imaginative temporary exhibitions it stages.

Eclectic collections Opened in 1950, the museum was the first art institution in the Miami area. A significant early benefactor was Samuel H. Kress, whose family bequeathed the substantial stock of predominantly Renaissance and baroque art that still provides the core of the permanent European holdings. Among many notable works on view are the 14th-century *Madonna and Child Enthroned With Donors and Saints Dominic and Elizabeth of Hungary*, by the Sienese Lippo Vanni; the entertaining 1650s *The Trapped Thief*, attributed to Van

The Lowe Art Museum has a fascinating collection of art from Europe and America

Galen; and works by later luminaries such as Thomas Gainsborough and Paul Gauguin.

American art A broad sweep of US art reaches from the 19th-century large-scale depictions of the American West by Albert Bierstadt and the mystically charged Florida landscapes of George Inness to modern works by Roy Liechtenstein and Duane Hanson, represented by Hanson's uncannily lifelike *College Football Player*. The Alfred I Barton Collection of Native American art includes some handsome Pueblo and Navajo weavings. Other noteworthy sights include a Haida halibut hook, made from wood and bone, a 19th-century Tlinglet frontlet headdress, a Zuni pueblo jar from around 1875 decorated with a deer design, and a set of imposing 1920s lithographs of Florida's Seminole chiefs.

THE BASICS

www.lowemuseum.org

➕ A9

✉ 1301 Stanford Drive, University of Miami

☎ 305/284-3535

🕐 Tue, Wed, Fri, Sat 10–5, Thu 12–7, Sun 12–5

🚊 University

🚌 48, 56, 152

♿ Good

💲 Moderate

Merrick House

Merrick House was the childhood home of Coral Gables architect George Merrick

THE BASICS

www.coralgables.com

+ A6

✉ 907 Coral Way

☎ 305/460-5361

🕐 Wed and Sun 1–4 or by appointment; gardens daily until dusk

🚌 24

♿ Few

💲 Moderate

HIGHLIGHTS

- Gardens
- Denman Fink's landscapes
- 1920s memorabilia

With his "City Beautiful" of Coral Gables, George Merrick achieved one of the most notable aesthetic successes of the 1920s Miami land boom. His boyhood home is an interesting stop for anyone intrigued by the architecture and by Merrick himself.

Early days In lush, tree-shaded gardens, the Coral Gables Merrick House dates from 1899 and began as a simple woodframe home for the Merrick family and an administrative base for running their citrus and vegetable farm. The farm flourished and the house expanded into the spacious residence of coral-rock walls topped with the red-tiled gabled roof that inspired the name of Merrick's great building project.

Looking inside An introductory video provides the background to the house and to George Merrick's later achievements, describing many of the distinguishing architectural features of the new city, some of which are represented in the house. Innumerable furnishings and ornaments, such as a grand piano and grandfather clock, are thought to be from the Merrick family's time, and the aging typewriter was used in farm correspondence. Many family photographs and enthusiastic, though amateurish, paintings by Mrs Merrick decorate the house. Economic hardship following the 1926 property crash caused the building to be converted into apartments known as Merrick Manor. Complete decline was halted only by its sale to a historically minded local in 1966 and the subsequent restoration program.

Venetian Pool

With its Venetian-style lamp posts, dainty cobblestoned bridges, cypress-roofed loggias, porticoes, palm trees and towers, few swimming pools anywhere in the world can match the architectural exuberance of the Venetian Pool.

Looking good The quarrying of rock to build Coral Gables during the 1920s left a very large hole in the ground, which, in keeping with the ingenuity that underpinned the creation of the city, was transformed into the majestic Venetian Pool. The pool was completed in 1924 and designed, like much of Coral Gables, by George Merrick's uncle, artist Denman Fink, and architect Phineas Paist. In its early years, the pool not only provided locals with a place to cool off but, with the drained pool functioning as an amphitheater, staged opera performances, beauty contests and concerts.

Making a splash Further entertainment was provided by the "water shows" of Olympic swimming gold medallist (and future Tarzan) Johnny Weissmuller and swimmer-actress Esther Williams, and the lectures given by the orator and former politician William Jennings Bryan. He praised Coral Gables to the skies in return for an annual salary of $50,000. The pool remains an extremely pleasant place to swim. Weekdays, outside school holidays, are particularly free of crowds. Until 1986, the pool was filled naturally from an artesian well, its 800,000 gallons (3 million liters) drained nightly and replaced each morning. Now, the water is recycled using natural ground filtration.

THE BASICS

🞦 A6
✉ 2701 De Soto Boulevard
☎ 305/460-5306
🕐 Jun–Aug daily; Sep–May Tue–Sun
🚌 24, 152
♿ Few
💲 Expensive/moderate (rate varies according to time of year)

HIGHLIGHTS

● Coral-rock waterfall (25ft/7.5m high)
● Photographs in the Rotunda Room
● Picnicking under the palm trees

More to See

CITY HALL
Financed by a bond issue, City Hall was completed in 1928 in a mere four months for a modest $200,000. The semicircular eastern wing, with its 12 columns supporting a cornice bearing the Coral Gables coat of arms, overlooks the business and shopping strip of the Miracle Mile. Emerging from the top of the pile is a three-tier Spanish Renaissance-style clock tower.
✚ B6 ✉ 405 Biltmore Way ☎ 305/446-6800 ◉ Best to visit Mon–Fri 9–5; closed holidays. Hours vary, call to check 🚌 24, 42, 56, J ⚫ Good ✋ Free

CORAL GABLES CONGREGATIONAL CHURCH
Completed in 1924, this pretty church has a Mediterranean style. Its 16th-century furniture is said to have been salvaged from shipwrecks.
✚ A6 ✉ 3010 De Soto Boulevard 🚌 152, J

CORAL GABLES TROLLEY
This electric trolley service follows a straight north-south route down Ponce de Leon Boulevard from SW 8th Street (Calle Ocho) down to the Village of Merrick Park shops and Douglas Road MetroRail station. There's a stop at the junction with the Miracle Mile.
✚ C7 ☎ 305/460-5070 ◉ Mon–Thu 6.30am–8pm, Fri 6.30am–10pm, every 10–15 mins ✋ Free

GRAND ENTRANCES, TOWERS AND FOUNTAINS
With his customary chutzpah, George Merrick planned eight grand entrances to his "City Beautiful." Four were built and three are easy to spot along SW 8th Street. The Douglas Entrance, or Puerto del Sol (Douglas Road), was intended as the entrance to a planned but never built Spanish Village. There is the vine-draped arch of the Granada Entrance (Granada Boulevard), based on the city gate of Granada, Spain, and the handsome pillars of the Country Club Prado Entrance (Country Club Prado). Also worth looking out for is the lovely De Soto fountain on Granada, near the Venetian Pool, and the lighthouse design that cloaks the Alhambra Water Tower (Alhambra Circle).

City Hall is listed on the National Register of Historic Places

The ornate bell tower of Coral Gables Congregational Church

Shopping

ALEXANDER AND VICTOR FINE ART

This sleek and spacious gallery displays contemporary paintings, sculpture and furnishings from around the world. Asian and European artists are well represented, alongside home-grown American talent. Check for details of special exhibitions and events.

✚ B6 ✉ 314 Miracle Mile ☎ 305/441-2324 🚌 24, 42, 56, J

BARNES & NOBLE

The many miles of shelving here are packed with fiction and nonfiction titles plus a formidable assortment of local, regional and a few international newspapers; an inviting café adjoins.

✚ C6 ✉ 152 Miracle Mile ☎ 305/446-4152 🚌 24, 42, 56, 152, J

BOOKS & BOOKS

Compact but very comprehensively stocked with general titles, an excellent selection of books about Miami, and books by Miami-based authors. Friendly staff will help you find what you need.

✚ C6 ✉ 265 Aragon Avenue ☎ 305/442-4408 🚌 24, 42, 56, J

BOY MEETS GIRL

Cool clothes for kids. Pick up the latest seasonal fashions for small people by the likes of Diesel, Lacoste and Small Paul, plus funky shoes by Naturino, and some really pretty girlie accessories.

✚ B6 ✉ 355 Miracle Mile ☎ 305/441-7173 🚌 24, 42, 56, 152, J

CORAL GABLES BRIDALS

Check out the sumptuous wedding outfits in shops along Coral Gables' Miracle Mile. This is just one among several bridal specialists filled with dazzling dresses, bridesmaid's outfits and other must-have creations and concoctions for the big day, including multitiered wedding cakes.

✚ C6 ✉ 141 Miracle Mile ☎ 305/445-5896 🚌 24, 42, 56, J

DOGBAR

Pooch pampering gone wild and just the place to find a little something for Fido if you're feeling a teensy bit guilty about that trip to the kennels …

STORYTIME

Younger children not smitten by Miami's charms might relish a few hours in one of the city's general bookstores that offer free storytelling sessions, sometimes with costumed characters narrating. Local newspapers have details about forthcoming events; those regularly staging such activities include the various branches of Books & Books and Barnes & Noble.

Perhaps a pink ballerina swimming cossie? A faux leopard-skin basket? Potions and lotions for healthy colons and bright eyes? Or a simple gourmet can of tinned lobster for dinner?

✚ B6 ✉ 259 Miracle Mile ☎ 305/441-8979 🚌 24, 42, 56, 152, J

SNOWS

Eschewing anything as vulgar as advertising, this top-of-the-range jewelry shop has built a deservedly excellent reputation through word of mouth since 1959.

✚ C6 ✉ 299 Miracle Mile ☎ 305/443-7448 🚌 24, 42, 56, J

VILLAGE OF MERRICK PARK

George Merrick would have approved of Coral Gables' latest upscale shopping enclave, with its attractive Mediterranean architecture, lush landscaping, palm trees and fountains. The Village is anchored by Neiman Marcus and Nordstrom, and offers a handsome collection of designer boutiques, galleries, jewelers and even an Elemis Spa, as well as restaurants and cafés catering for the ladies who lunch.

✚ B/C8 ✉ 358 San Lorenzo Avenue (LeJeune Road/ SW 42nd Avenue) ☎ 305/461-2311 🚌 40, 42, 56, 152, J

Entertainment and Nightlife

ACTORS' PLAYHOUSE AT THE MIRACLE THEATRE

From Broadway spectaculars to more introspective offerings, this splendidly restored art deco theater mounts varied fare in its 600-seat main hall.

➕ C6 ✉ 280 Miracle Mile ☎ 305/444-9293 🚌 24, 42, 56, J

CAFÉ AT BOOKS & BOOKS

Glass of wine in hand, enjoy free live music (it's generally jazz) in the courtyard on Friday evenings.

➕ C6 ✉ 265 Aragon Avenue (at Ponce de Leon Boulevard) ☎ 305/442-4408 🚌 24, 42, 56, J

FROST SCHOOL OF MUSIC

The university music school's 600-seat venue has excellent acoustics and hosts opera, choral and chamber music by students and visiting musicians.

➕ A9 ✉ 1314 Miller Drive ☎ 305/284-2438 🚇 University 🚌 48, 56, 152

GABLE STAGE AT THE BILTMORE

This gem of a theater, inside the historic Biltmore Hotel (▷ 64), is home of the highly regarded Florida Shakespeare Theater, now known as Gable Stage, which mounts several major productions each year in this intimate

154-seat auditorium. It also hosts contemporary productions and Florida premieres of Tony Award-winning productions.

➕ A7 ✉ Biltmore Hotel, 1200 Anastasia Avenue ☎ 305/445-1119 🚌 152

THE GLOBE CAFÉ

This sleek café and bar is packed with bright, young, moneyed creatures. Enjoy a meal from the pan-bistro type menu (pasta, steak, seafood), or just pitch up for the vibe, with live new music showcases on Wednesday and jazz on Saturday.

➕ B6 ✉ 377 Alhambra Circle (at LeJeune Road/SW 42nd Avenue) ☎ 305/445-3555 🚌 24, 42, 56, J

JERRY HERMAN RING THEATER

The University of Miami's major dramatic space hosts student and professional shows, and deserving works by lesser-known playwrights.

➕ A9 ✉ 1312 Miller Drive ☎ 305/284-3355 🚇 University 🚌 48, 56, 57

JOHNMARTIN'S PUB

The sideroom of an Irish restaurant serves stouts and ales across a handsome mahogany bar.

➕ C6 ✉ 253 Miracle Mile ☎ 305/445-3777 🚌 24, 42, J

NEW THEATRE

A comfortable venue with a mixed repertoire of classical and contemporary productions, plus a few comedies.

➕ B7 ✉ 4120 Laguna Street ☎ 305/443-5909 🚌 42, 56, 152, J

TITANIC BREWERY AND RESTAURANT

A frat-pack haunt across the street from the university, but the food is good, the home-brewed ales are diverse (Belgian-style pale ales, German rye brews and English Best Bitter) and regularly pick up awards, and there's live music on Friday and Saturday nights (rock, R&B) and a Blues Jam on Wednesday.

➕ Off map ✉ 5813 Ponce de Leon Boulevard (at San Amaro Drive) ☎ 305/667-2537 🚇 Metrorail University 🚌 48, 56, 57, 152

Restaurants

Prices are approximate, based on a three-course meal for one person.
$$$ over $40
$$ $20–$40
$ under $20

BRASSERIE LES HALLES ($$)

This brasserie dishes up French classics, from garlicky snails and onion soup to *steak au poivre* and mouth-watering tarte Tatin.

➕ C6 ✉ 2415 Ponce de Leon (at Miracle Mile) ☎ 305/461-1099 🚌 24, 42, 56, 224, J

CAFFÈ ABBRACCI ($$$)

Celebrities and power diners head for this stylish Italian *ristorante* in the Gables. Excellent veal and homemade carpaccio.

➕ B6 ✉ 318 Aragon Avenue ☎ 305/441-0700 🕐 Dinner only Sat and Sun 🚌 42, J

CHEF INNOCENT AT ST. MICHEL ($$–$$$)

This fine French-rooted restaurant and steak house is in intimate, romantic surroundings in a restored 1920s hotel.

➕ B6 ✉ 162 Alcazar Avenue ☎ 305/446-6572 🚌 42

CHISPA ($$–$$$)

The preferred Coral Gables haunt of YUCAS (Young Urban Cuban Americans), Chispa is lively and cool. Great Nuevo Latino cooking

with a creative touch—shrimp and pork spring rolls, corn-based pizza topped with pork, figs and blue cheese—don't miss the guava cheesecake.

➕ C7 ✉ 225 Altara Avenue (at Aurora Street) ☎ 305/648-2600 🚌 40, 42, 56, 152, J

HOUSE OF INDIA ($–$$)

A long-standing Gables favorite. The space is a clutter but the lunch buffet is excellent value. Breads from the tandoori oven are delicious, as are the goat and the spinach and lamb curries.

➕ Off map ✉ 22 Merrick Way (Coral Way at SW 37th Avenue) ☎ 305/444-2348 🕐 Dinner only Sun 🚌 24, 37, 224

NEW FLORIDIAN CUISINE

Food critics are excited about the innovative dishes created by Miami-based American chefs using the extraordinary range of produce from the Caribbean and Central America (Floribbean fare). These innovators conjure up exciting and picturesque dishes, featuring regional fish and exotic fruits, vegetables and spices. Cindy Hutson at Ortanique (▷ above), Allan Susser and Mark Militello are the chief exponents, imitated by increasing numbers of enthusiastic followers.

EL NOVILLO ($$–$$$)

One of Miami's highly regarded Nicaraguan restaurants, El Novillio is especially popular for its *churrasco* (grilled steak).

➕ Off map ✉ 6830 Bird Road (SW 40th Street), west of Coral Gables ☎ 305/284-8417 🚌 40

ORTANIQUE ON THE MILE ($$$)

Chic, island-inspired decor makes the perfect setting for Floribbean cuisine. Sample mussels cooked in a coconut curry broth, lobster with mango, or black grouper spiked with orange liqueur and lemon rum—as well as jerk chicken pasta and fruity desserts.

➕ B6 ✉ 278 Miracle Mile (at LeJeune/SW 42nd Avenue) ☎ 305/446-7710 🕐 Mon–Tue lunch, dinner; Sat, Sun dinner 🚌 24, 42, 56, 152, J

PALME D'OR ($$$)

French-trained chef Philippe Ruiz brings a distinctive flair to the fine-dining experience at the Biltmore. There are Spanish/Caribbean notes to the perfectly executed appetizer-size plates, which build up to three-, four- or five-course prix-fixe meals. The menu includes unforgettably intense Maine lobster cappuccino; asparagus and parmesan beignets and a weighty wine list.

➕ A7 ✉ 1200 Anastasia Avenue ☎ 305/445-1926 🚌 152

A history of pioneers, Bahamian immigrants, writers, artists and their flower-children successors of the 1960s and '70s permeates laidback Coconut Grove. Beyond the Grove's bustling, villagey heart is exclusive, beach-fringed Key Biscayne.

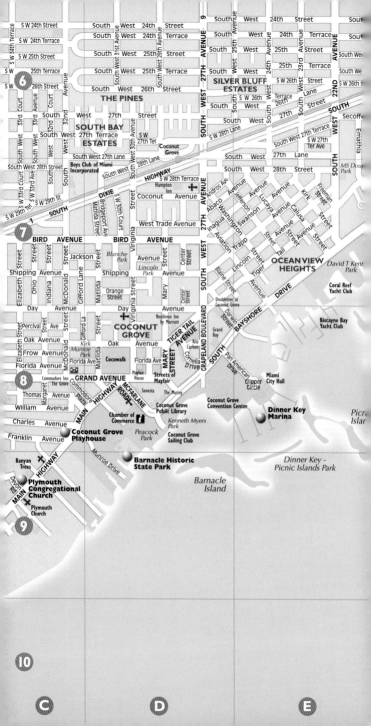

Map labels

24th Street
24th Terrace
South West 19th Avenue
South West 24th Avenue
Street
Terrace
HIGHWAY
Wakeena Drive
C-A-Tee Dr
Opechee Drive
Espanola Drive
Secoffee Street
Nethia Drive
Hilola Street
Noc-A-Tee Drive
Onaway Drive
Tall Avenue
Micanopy Avenue
Tiger Avenue
Natoma Street
Tall
17TH
AVENUE
South West 1st Avenue
WEST
SOUTH
SOUTH
BAYSHORE
DRIVE
Crystal Court
Coacoochee Street
Crystal View Court
Ah-We-Wa Street
Fairisle
Cristal Isle
West Trade Street
West Glencoe
East Glencoe
Fairlisle
Fairhaven Place
South Bayshore Lane
Bayshore Village
Bayshore Drive

Shore Drive West
Bay Heights Drive
Shore Drive South
Pinta Road
Alika Avenue
BAY HEIGHTS
MIAMI AVENUE
Shore Drive East
Drive

Eco Adventure Kayak and Snorkeling Tours, Hobie Island, Stiltsville

Miami Science Museum

Bill Baggs Cape Florida SRA, Crandon Beach Park, Miami Seaquarium

Vizcaya Museum and Gardens

Ermita de la Caridad

Heliport

Grove Isle Club and Resort

Fair Isle / Grove Isle

Biscayne Bay

```
0        250 m
0        250 yds
```

F

G

Barnacle Historic State Park

TOP 25

The Barnacle (left); view of boats from the Barnacle dock (right)

THE BASICS

www.floridastateparks.org/thebarnacle

✚ D9

✉ 3485 Main Highway

☎ 305/442-6866

◉ Fri–Mon 9–4; guided tours 10, 11.30, 1 and 2.30

🚌 48

♿ Few

💷 Inexpensive

HIGHLIGHTS

● Spotting native flora and fauna in the hardwood hammock

● Early pioneer photographs

● Antique furnishings

Few pioneer dwellings are as ingenious or as well preserved as the Barnacle, erected by a sea-loving Massachusetts boat designer and Miami pioneer who was described as "the catalyst that brought Coconut Grove into being."

Arrival Ralph Middleton Munroe, a naval architect and photographer, first visited the area in 1881, hoping the climate would help his wife, Eva, ill with tuberculosis. He befriended Charles and Isabella Peacock, future owners of Miami's first hotel, who gave him 4 acres (1.6ha) of land. In 1891 Munroe returned permanently, buying a further 40 acres (16ha) on which to build his bayside home.

Settlement Munroe earned a national reputation designing shallow-draft vessels for the treacherous waters around Florida's coast. With the Barnacle, he also showed considerable skills in domestic building. Raised above ground to improve air flow and prevent flooding, the Barnacle has a veranda to provide shade and shelter, and a skylight to improve air circulation. Coated with oil to deter termites, the pine posts that anchor the Barnacle to the ground also helped it survive the hurricanes of 1926 and 1992. Most ingeniously of all, Munroe created extra living space in 1908 by raising the Barnacle above ground and building an extra floor under the original one. Insulated from the highway by a dense tropical hardwood hammock and furnished with family heirlooms, the house is a veritable time capsule of early Coconut Grove life.

The Cape Florida lighthouse, rebuilt in 1845

Bill Baggs Cape Florida SRA

A sandy beach bathed in Florida sunshine and the slow "drawl of the sea" so evocatively described by newspaper editor Bill Baggs are just two of the reasons to venture down to this unspoiled beach park at the southern tip of Key Biscayne.

Hurricane damage The 494-acre (200ha) park occupies the lower third of Key Biscayne, stretching from the bayside to the ocean and narrowing to a tip guarded by the Cape Florida lighthouse. It is named for a former editor of the *Miami News*, whose campaign to protect the peninsula from development led to the creation of the park in 1967. In 1992, the eye of Hurricane Andrew passed right over Cape Florida, decimating the park's woodlands, uprooting non-native species and clearing the way for a restoration project that has reintroduced all-native species to the board-walk-accessible maritime hammock, the mangrove-edged tidal swamp areas and the dunes. Native animals and birds have also returned, including American crocodiles, while loggerhead turtles nest on the Atlantic beach during summer.

Seminole attack The park's most famous landmark is the 95ft (29m) Cape Florida lighthouse, the oldest standing structure in Miami-Dade County (guided tours). The original 1825 structure was destroyed during the Seminole Wars and rebuilt in 1845. Climb the 109 steps for spectacular views over the bay and off to Stiltsville (▷ 85), followed by a short film and a visit to the Keeper's Cottage, furnished with memorabilia.

THE BASICS

www.floridastateparks.org/capeflorida/

✚ Off map at G6

✉ 1200 S Crandon Boulevard, Key Biscayne

☎ 305/361-5811

🕐 8am–dusk. Lighthouse tours Thu–Mon 10am, 1pm

🍴 Cafés

🚌 B

♿ Few

💲 Inexpensive

HIGHLIGHTS

● Lighthouse tour
● Renting a bike and exploring the nature trails
● Renting a beach chair and umbrella and snoozing the day away
● Bird-watching in the mangrove wetlands

TIP

● Sign up early for the light-house tour as there are only 10 places per tour.

Miami Science Museum

World-class visiting exhibitions are the highlight at the Miami Science Museum

THE BASICS

www.miamisci.org

⊕ G6

✉ 3280 S Miami Avenue

☎ 305/646-4200

🕐 Daily 10–6

🚇 Vizcaya

🚌 48

♿ Very good

💲 Expensive

HIGHLIGHTS

● Snakes
● Giant tortoises
● Exhibitions
● Collections Gallery
● Planetarium
● Birds of prey

Since its founding in 1949, the Miami Science Museum and Space Transit Planetarium has been exploring some of the mysteries and wonders of the natural world through its hands-on exhibits, small Wildlife Center and Planetarium.

Permanent exhibits In truth, the permanent galleries are looking pretty tired these days and the museum is slated for a move to the Museum Park being created on the Downtown bayfront, due to open in 2011. However, do check the schedules as this museum's strength is attracting eye-popping, world-class visiting exhibitions. Investigations into sound, light and gravity, dioramas of natural Florida, and displays on ocean life form the core of the permanent exhibits. The geological specimens, such as fossilized sharks' teeth, the snake exhibit and skewered creepie-crawlies, are always popular, and maybe an astronomy show at the Planetarium, which also hosts laser spectaculars. Outside in the Wildlife Center, there are giant tortoises, baby alligators and rescued raptors being nursed back to recovery.

Visiting marvels The museum's ability to pull in major visiting exhibitions can be put down to a fruitful affiliation with the Smithsonian Institution in Washington, DC. In recent years, visiting exhibits have included the extraordinary *Dinosaurs of China*, a world debut for a collection containing 14 mounted dinosaur skeletons and 52 real dinosaur fossils, lent by the Museum of Beijing, China.

Meet the dolphins (left) and the killer whale Lolita (right) at Miami Seaquarium

Miami Seaquarium

COCONUT GROVE AND KEY BISCAYNE

TOP 25

Founded in 1955, the Seaquarium is one of Miami's hardy perennials. This pleasingly small-scale marine park is big on shows and offers just enough alternative attractions to be easily manageable in half a day.

Showtime It all began with Flipper, the bottlenose dolphin star of the 1960s TV series, which was filmed at the park. Ever since, the crowds have been packing the bleachers to marvel at the antics of the Seaquarium's highly trained marine performers as they leap and dive their way through astonishing tricks and stunts guaranteed to impress even the most jaded observer. To get the best out of the Seaquarium, plot your visit around the show schedule and then fill in the time between shows with side attractions. The absolute must-see spectacular is the Killer Whale and Dolphin Show, starring five-ton Lolita, the killer whale. She makes the biggest splash in the park, so avoid the first few rows unless you want a serious drenching. The dolphin shows are full of ooohs and aaahs, and the sea lions ham it up with gusto.

Conservation The Seaquarium has been at the forefront of marine conservation for decades, undertaking breeding programs and rescuing injured animals. The park's manatees are all rescued and bear the scars of their injuries. There are also reef and bird exhibits, tropical fish aquariums, alligators, turtles and the Shark Channel, full of circling sharks waiting for their next feed.

THE BASICS

www.miamiseaquarium.com
🔷 Off map at G6
✉ 4400 Rickenbacker Causeway
☎ 305/361-5705
🕐 Daily 9.30–6
🍴 Cafés
🅱 B
♿ Good
👍 Expensive

HIGHLIGHTS

● Killer Whale and Dolphin Show
● Golden Dome Sea Lion Show
● Top Deck Dolphin Show
● Manatee Exhibit
● Shark feeding
● Water cannons at Salty's
● Pirate Playground

81

Vizcaya Museum and Gardens

HIGHLIGHTS

- Music Room
- Renaissance Hall
- Tea Room
- Breakfast Room
- Adams Library
- Banquet Hall
- Deering Bedroom
- Gardens

TIP

- Allow plenty of time to enjoy the 10-acre (4ha) Italian and French gardens.

It must have looked like a mirage to the very first guests arriving by boat for Christmas 1916: an Italian-Renaissance villa transplanted to Miami's mangrove-lined bayshore, complete with antique furnishings and art collections.

Authenticity Northern industrialist James Deering developed a liking for winter in Florida, and thought nothing of spending $15 million on his monumental pied-à-terre on Biscayne Bay. Together with architect F. Burrall Hoffman and artistic supervisor Paul Chafin, Deering traveled widely in Italy, studying 16th-century architecture and filling crate after crate with art treasures to add authenticity to a villa that he hoped would look as though it had been inhabited for 400 years. At a time when Miami's population was 10,000,

The Italianate house and grounds of Vizcaya Museum and Gardens

around 1,000 people worked on the building of Vizcaya. After its completion (in a mere two years), a small army stayed on as servants, gardeners and handymen. Rooms were designed in a mixture of styles to reflect the fashions of different eras. Nonetheless, Vizcaya's diverse strands, Italian Renaissance, baroque, rococo and neoclassical, come together with surprising cohesion.

By boat Deering's dinner guests arrived by gondola, navigating the Venetian-style Great Stone Barge on Biscayne Bay. Today's visitors enter from the land side, greeted by a statue of Bacchus from where guided tours depart. These are essential in understanding a house whose 34 rooms each hold decorative treasures and anecdotal interest, alongside innovations in domestic architecture such as elevators.

THE BASICS

www.vizcayamuseum.org

⊕ G6

✉ 3251 S Miami Avenue

☎ 305/250-9133

🕐 Daily 9.30–4.30

🍴 Café

🚇 Vizcaya

🚌 48

♿ Good

💰 Expensive

More to See

COCONUT GROVE PLAYHOUSE

This attractive 1920s Mediterranean-style theater was originally a cinema. Showing live drama since the 1960s, the Playhouse earned national kudos by staging the first US production of Samuel Beckett's *Waiting For Godot*.

➕ C8 ✉ 3500 Main Highway, Coconut Grove ☎ 305/442-4000 🚇 Coconut Grove 🚌 48

CRANDON BEACH PARK

A 3-mile (5km) swathe of golden-sand, oceanfront beach shaded by coconut palms makes Crandon Park one of Miami's most popular week-end spots for sunbathing, swimming and beach barbecues. Come during the week, however, and you could have the place almost to yourself.

➕ Off map at G6 ✉ 4000 Crandon Boulevard, Key Biscayne 🚌 B

DINNER KEY MARINA

Start/finish point of the Columbus Day Regatta (October), this was where early Grove residents set out on boating expeditions, hence the name. Today you can admire the art deco Miami City Hall, originally the Pan Am seaplane terminal, visit water-front bars and rent charter boats.

➕ E8 ✉ 3400 Pan American Drive, Coconut Grove 🚌 48

ECO-ADVENTURE KAYAK AND SNORKELING TOURS

www.miamidade.gov/parks/ecoadventures

Kayak tours are a great way to get out and about on Biscayne Bay. The sheltered seagrass beds in Crandon Park's Bear Cut Marine Preserve are home to all manner of tropical fish, conchs, rays and other sea creatures. Another tour heads out to Pelican Harbor in the north bay area.

➕ Off map at G6 ✉ 4000 Crandon Boulevard, Key Biscayne ☎ 305/365-3018 🚌 B

ERMITA DE LA CARIDAD

On the bayshore, its altar aligned with distant Cuba, this unusual modern church is deeply symbolic to Miami's Cuban population. It dates from 1966, and was paid for by 10-cent donations from the community.

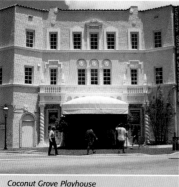

Coconut Grove Playhouse

Luxury yachts in Dinner Key Marina

Its shrine is dedicated to Cuba's patron saint, the Virgin of Charity, depicted in a mural inside.

⊞ G6 ✉ 3609 South Miami Avenue, Bay Heights ☎ 305/854-2404 🚌 48

HOBIE ISLAND

The beaches on the south side of the Rickenbacker Causeway, between the mainland and Key Biscayne, are narrow and shingly but are popular with catamaran and windsurf enthusiasts. Equipment rental is available. Jetskis ply the waters north of the causeway.

⊞ Off map at G6

PLYMOUTH CONGREGATIONAL CHURCH

The origins of the church reach back to 1897, when the isolated settlement of Coconut Grove was served by a small wooden chapel. By 1916 the current coral rock structure was under construction, loosely modeled on a city mission church in Mexico, with a tall portico and twin bell towers. The stonework was completed by a lone Spanish mason, using no tools other than a T-square, hatchet, trowel and plumb line. The main entrance is an oak-backed walnut door with wrought-iron fittings that originally belonged to a monastery in the Pyrenees.

⊞ C9 ✉ 3400 Devon Road ☎ 305/444-6521 🕐 Hours vary, but the church can be unlocked for visits; telephone before arrival 🚌 48 ♿ Few 🆓 Free

STILTSVILLE

One more sizeable hurricane and the last fragile remains of Stiltsville will probably disappear for good, gently floating off on the tide. This rickety but appealing collection of stilted houses perched in the bay is a much-loved local landmark and focus of an impassioned campaign to preserve the last seven structures. Originally a cluster of fish camps, boat clubs and weekend retreats, Stiltsville's slightly anarchic reputation has attracted the ire of the local authorities for decades and restrictions on repairs have virtually assured the settlement's demise in the very near future.

⊞ Off map at G6

Plymouth Congregational Church, with its twin bell towers

Coconut Grove

This short amble down Main Highway leads to a clutch of Coconut Grove's most historic buildings.

DISTANCE: 1 mile (0.6km) **ALLOW:** 1 hour

START

MAIN HIGHWAY at Grand Avenue
🚇 D8 🚌 48, 249

❶ With Coconut Walk behind you, start walking down Main Highway, browsing in the shops and deciding which sidewalk café you'll stop at on the return route. Two of the best cafés for a reviving drink or lunch on Main Highway are the Greenstreet Café (▷ 90) and Le Bouchon du Grove (3430 Main Highway).

❷ At the corner with Charles Avenue, the Coconut Grove Playhouse (▷ 84) is a splendid 1920s affair, liberally decorated with curly barleysugar columns, pediments and balustrades, all picked out in white for maximum effect.

❸ Charles Avenue was the Grove's original Bahamian settlement, with wooden homes, or "conch houses," more commonly found in the Florida Keys. This rundown area is known as the Black Grove, set in uncomfortable proximity to its wealthy neighbor.

END

MAIN HIGHWAY at Grand Avenue
🚇 D8 🚌 48, 249

❻ From the church, retrace your steps back toward the heart of the Grove, stopping at the Barnacle Historic State Park (▷ 78) for a glimpse of how Coconut Grove looked in pioneer days. The driveway winds through the hammock and the grounds lead all the way down to the bay.

❺ At Devon Road, the red-tiled roof of the Plymouth Congregational Church (▷ 85) is visible on the right. Cross Main Highway with care to inspect this handsome mission-style building and several lovely old homes set in a quiet residential enclave.

❹ Cross Main Highway, and continue along the sidewalk bordered by a tangle of native hardwood hammock. The arterial roots of magnificent ancient banyan trees have bored their way into the soft coral rock walls of former bayfront estates, while the peeling, red bark of the gumbo limbos earns them their local nickname "tourist trees."

Shopping

COCOWALK

Once hailed as the Savior of Coconut Grove, this terraced conglomeration of restaurants and shops is all pretty predictable and full of mainstream stores and eateries these days. However, it is at its liveliest and most enjoyable on busy weekends. There's also a cinema complex.

➕ D8 ✉ 3015 Grand Avenue, Coconut Grove ☎ 305/444-0777 🚇 Coconut Grove 🚌 48, 249

THE FASHIONISTA

The Fashionista is a small but interesting consignment boutique offering good-condition, secondhand designer clothes and accessories from the likes of YSL, Dolce & Gabbana and others.

➕ C–D8 ✉ 3138 Commodore Plaza, Coconut Grove ☎ 305/443-4331 🚌 48, 249

GROVE'S GALLERY

Come here for wacky and, in some cases, wearable art in all sorts of mediums, from paintings, prints, sculpture and jewelry to creations by Carlos & Albert. The latter are large and vibrant Mexican-influenced animals made from papier-mâché, fiberglass or pottery.

➕ C8 ✉ 3137 Commodore Plaza, Coconut Grove ☎ 305/444-2900 🚌 48, 249

JAKE'S GROVE

If you're after good-quality cotton casualwear, try Jake's Grove, whose motto is "Life is good." Their T-shirts, sweats, shorts, baseball caps and footwear are indeed pretty good and the kids' clothes are cute, too.

➕ D8 ✉ 2994 MacFarlane Road, Coconut Grove ☎ 305/529-6526 🚌 48, 249

MAUI NIX

This well-stocked surfie emporium has all the usual suspects gathered under one roof: Rip Curl, Billabong, Quiksilver and the rest. Choose from cool tees, boardshorts, must-have beach bags,

SOUVENIR HUNTING

Miami is a glorious repository of all that is best–or possibly worst, depending on your taste– about Florida souvenir hunting. South Beach is the unassailable capital of tongue-in-cheek shops awash with Floridiana in all its palm tree, flamingo and alligator motif splendor. The Bayside Marketplace and Coconut Grove run a close second and third. For something a little less tacky, check out Lincoln Road's Antiques and Collectibles Market, which takes place on the second and fourth Sunday of the month.

eyewear and a selection of kid's stuff, including delectable little hula shorts for wannabe Hawaiian hula dancers.

➕ D8 ✉ CocoWalk, 3015 Grand Avenue, Coconut Grove ☎ 305/444-6919 🚌 48, 249

PALM PRODUCE RESORTWEAR

This is the perfect place to find that little beach-wrap, light cool trousers or a loose tie-front cotton shawl for the evening. There's everything you need to make your tan look spectacular and some great pastel-hue cotton grandad shirts for the boys, too.

➕ D8 ✉ CocoWalk, 3015 Grand Avenue, Coconut Grove ☎ 305/445-5533 🚌 48, 249

STREETS OF MAYFAIR

Patterned tiles, fountains and assorted statuary create a Mediterranean mood at this mazelike three-building collection of chic boutiques, art galleries and other diversions for the well-heeled. Come evening, attention switches to its cluster of eateries, nightclubs and entertainment venues (▷ Cielo Garden and Improv, 88).

➕ D8 ✉ 2911 Grand Avenue, Coconut Grove ☎ 305/448-1700 🚇 Coconut Grove 🚌 48, 249

Entertainment and Nightlife

3484 MAIN HIGHWAY

This bar-restaurant has a broad-ranging musical menu. Check schedules, but the end of the week follows a fairly regular diet of hip-hop Thursday, rock Friday, Global Lounge Saturday and open mike Sunday.

⊞ C8 ⊠ 3484 Main Highway, Coconut Grove ☎ 305/445-0022 🚌 48, 249

AMADEUS

If you find Miami's Latin vibe getting to you, Tango Tuesday at the atmospheric Amadeus bar in the Ritz Carlton is the place to learn to tango. The class is at 9pm, and then you can try out your new moves afterward with dancing until closing time. Dress is smart-casual.

⊞ D8 ⊠ Ritz Carlton Hotel, 3300 SW 27 Avenue, Coconut Grove ☎ 305/644-4680 🚌 22, 27, 48, 249

CIELO GARDEN

A deservedly popular restaurant and Cuban-style lounge combining good, beautifully presented food with Latin music acts most nights. The decor is amazing—all low blue lights transforming beaded curtains into sparkly waterfalls of glass set behind stark white sofas and a sinuous bar.

⊞ D8 ⊠ Streets of Mayfair, 3390 Mary Street, Coconut Grove ☎ 305/446-9060 🚌 48, 249

COCONUT GROVE PLAYHOUSE

See page 84.

FAT TUESDAY

Frozen daiquiris, happy hours and other cut-price deals fuel a boisterous crowd. Part of the chain.

⊞ D8 ⊠ CocoWalk, 3015 Grand Avenue, Coconut Grove ☎ 305/441-2992 🔘 Coconut Grove 🚌 48, 249

FLAVOUR

The Grove's biggest club is spread over two floors in a former Masonic temple. Rock, retro, freestyle and house, plus a spot of dining and lounging, keep a relatively dressy crowd happy. Feeling more down-at-heel? Try the midweek

---

GROVE FESTIVALS

Coconut Grove's fun-packed festival calendar begins with Taste of the Grove, a foodie event with live music in Peacock Park in January. In February, it's the Coconut Grove Arts Festival, when talented artists and unknown amateurs display their works along Bayshore Drive. The lively Goombay Festival draws thousands of revelers to a Bahamian-style carnival in early June; and the year is seen out by the King Mango Strut street parade on New Year's Eve.

---

pool and juke-box session on Wednesdays.

⊞ D8 ⊠ 2895 MacFarlane Road, Coconut Grove ☎ 305/445-6511 🚌 48, 249

IMPROV

Long-standing comedy club and dinner theater tucked away in the Streets of Mayfair complex.

⊞ D8 ⊠ Streets of Mayfair, 3390 Mary Street, Coconut Grove ☎ 305/441-8200 🚌 48, 249

MR. MOE'S

This sports bar dishes up groaning platters of BBQ, televised games (beware of Miami Hurricanes football clashes, unless you fancy drowning in a sea of orange and green) and endless jugs of beer. There's live music from Thursday to Saturday, when they may also wheel out the mechanical bull for those too beered-up to know better.

⊞ C–D8 ⊠ 3131 Commodore Plaza, Coconut Grove ☎ 305/442-1114 🚌 48, 249

OXYGEN LANDING

The home of the terminally hip in the Grove and the nearest thing you'll find to a SoBe lounge in this neck of the woods. Dimly-lit subterranean lounge and sushi bar, plus sounds ranging from hip-hop and house to Latin salsa and merengue.

⊞ D8 ⊠ 2911 Grand Avenue, Coconut Grove ☎ 305/476-0202 🚌 48, 249

Restaurants

PRICES

Prices are approximate, based on a three-course meal for one person.

$$$	over $40
$$	$20–$40
$	under $20

BALEEN ($$$)

Enjoy innovative seafood dishes at this glamorous restaurant on the water. Call ahead to reserve a table on the terrace.

✚ F–G7 ✉ Grove Isle Resort, 4 Grove Isle Drive, Coconut Grove
☎ 305/858-8300 🚌 48

LE BOUCHON DU GROVE ($$–$$$)

The setting may be more Miami than Marseilles, but the sensibilities are entirely Gallic at this bustling French bistro. Grab a sidewalk seat and order up a café-croissant for breakfast, or maybe *moules frites* with a glass of wine for lunch. At cocktail hour it's a kir royale and then blow the diet with a succulent *confit de canard*.

✚ D8 ✉ 3430 Main Highway, Coconut Grove
☎ 305/448-6060 🚌 48, 249

FOCACCIA ($)

Great little corner bakery and café serving tasty sandwiches and salads, or a breakfast croissant with scrambled eggs to start the day. The French pastries are fabulous—the *pain au chocolat* could have come from Paris—and artisan breads. Yum.

✚ C8 ✉ 3111 Grand Avenue, Coconut Grove
☎ 305/476-8292 🚫 Closed Sun 🚌 48, 249

GREENSTREET CAFÉ ($$)

One of the first sidewalk cafés in the Grove, Greenstreet attracts local movers and shakers with its eclectic menu and front-row views of the street parade. There are great salads, pasta, lamb burgers with goat's cheese, a kids' menu and charming waitstaff. The dark, plush interior has chandeliers, huge mirrors and marble-topped tables balanced on iron lion's paw legs.

✚ D8 ✉ 3468 Main Highway, Coconut Grove
☎ 305/444-0244 🚌 48, 249

SEAFOOD

The most avidly consumed local dish is the claws of the stone crab, a large, creamy and chewy crustacean in season from mid-October to mid-May and often very expensive. Other delights include Florida lobster and conch (pronounced 'konk'), which is commonly served in fritters and chowders. Among popular fish are grouper, tuna, swordfish and dolphin (as mahimahi is known here), often served grilled or blackened Southern style.

MONTY'S STONE CRAB RESTAURANT ($$$)

The original branch of the noted seafood eatery, now also in South Beach, has a prime position on the edge of the marina and its reputation for stone crabs is fully justified.

✚ E7 ✉ 2550 S Bayshore Drive, Coconut Grove
☎ 305/856-3992 🚌 48

RUSTY PELICAN ($$–$$$)

The view is the big draw to this waterfront institution, with its sweeping vistas across Biscayne Bay to the Downtown skyline. You pay rather less to enjoy it with a drink on the terrace, but the steak and seafood menu is solid and reliable.

✚ Off map ✉ 3201 Rickenbacker Causeway, Virginia Key ☎ 305/361-3818
🚌 B

SCOTTY'S LANDING ($–$$)

Generous, no-nonsense seafood and juicy burgers served up on the dock by the City Hall, with the clatter of rigging jangling in the salty air, plastic table and chairs and prices to warm the cockles of your wallet. Enjoy hearty chowders, delicious grilled fish sandwiches, and very cold beer.

✚ E8 ✉ 3381 Pan American Drive, Coconut Grove
☎ 305/854-2626 🚌 48, 249

From coral reefs and animals to botanic gardens and railroad history, most of the more distant attractions are spread throughout South Miami, the sprawling suburbs bordering the Everglades National Park and the island-hopping road to the Florida Keys.

Farther Afield

Biscayne National Park

HIGHLIGHTS

● Dolphins playing in the wake of the glass-bottomed boat (no guarantees)
● Kayaking in the back bay and watching rays swimming in the Shallow Jones Lagoon
● Playing Robinson Crusoe with a picnic and a good book on Elliott Key

TIP

● Call ahead to check boat trip and tour schedules, as things change according to the weather and the season.

Way down south of the city, near the start of the Florida Keys, Biscayne National Park extends over a vast 172,000-acre (69,000ha) preserve, 96 percent of which is underwater and can be explored only by boat, snorkeling or diving.

Marine magic The park encompasses the southern reaches of Biscayne Bay and the northern tip of the world's third-largest coral reef, a magical submarine world that trails down the Florida Keys island chain for some 100 miles (160km). The reef's abundant sea creatures include around 500 species of fish, while manatees and crocodiles shelter in the lee of dozens of green islets scattered across the shallow bay. The Dante Fascell Visitor Center at the Convoy Point headquarters is a good place to get an overview of the park.

There are many ways to explore Biscayne National Park, whether you prefer to be on board a boat, strolling along the boardwalk, snorkeling, canoeing or scuba-diving

There are exhibits, a touch table and rangers on hand to answer any questions. Boat tours also depart from Convoy Point, providing transportation out to the reef and spectacular views of corals, tropical fish and sea turtles.

Below the waves Things get even better beneath the waves, with close-up encounters out on the reef and around the richly populated mangrove-lined shore. Snorkeling trips are available daily, and certified scuba divers can reserve a two-tank dive on weekends. To get out on the water unaccompanied and explore the maze of islands and lagoons, rent a canoe or kayak, and there is a basic campsite on Elliott Key. Pick a really calm day to take the glass-bottomed boat trip for the best possible visibility; the view will be murky if it's windy and the sea is choppy.

THE BASICS

✚ Off map to south
✉ Convoy Point HQ: Canal Drive, off SW 328th Street (east of Homestead and US1)
☎ HQ: 305/230-7275
🕐 Underwater area: 24 hours. Convoy Point HQ: 7am–5.30pm. Visitor Center: 9am–5pm
💵 Free
♿ Few
⛴ Glass-bottomed boat trips daily 10am (3 hours); less frequent excursions to Elliott and Boca Chita Keys. Snorkeling trips (reserve ahead) daily 1.30pm (3 hours); scuba trips (reserve ahead) Sat, Sun 8.30am (4.5 hours). Reservations: ☎ 305/230-1100

Fairchild Tropical Botanic Garden

See tropical plants and beautiful lakes at the Fairchild Tropical Botanic Garden

THE BASICS

www.fairchildgarden.org
➕ Off map to south
✉ 10901 Old Cutler Road
☎ 305/667-1651
🕐 Daily 9.30–4.30
🍴 Café
🚌 65
♿ Good
💲 Expensive
❓ Many weekend special events

HIGHLIGHTS

● Guide-led tours for extra insight
● The fern collection
● Exotic plants in the Window to the Tropics hot house, notably the orchid collection

Southern Florida is the only place in the continental United States where subtropical and tropical plants can grow outdoors year-round, and these 83-acre (34ha) gardens display an astounding wealth of native and exotic species.

Germination Built during the Depression by the Civilian Conservation Corps (CCC), the Fairchild Tropical Botanic Garden has been open to the public since 1938. The gardens bear the name of distinguished botanist David Fairchild, a resident of Miami whose life's work was to bring examples of tropical plants to the United States, and they not only showcase plantlife but also run numerous educational programs. Miles of pathway weave through the gardens beside beautiful lakes, and a useful overview is provided by the 40-minute narrated tram tour, which is included in the admission price.

Tropical scents Among the wealth of palms, bromeliads, cycads, vines and much more, are oddities such as the massive African baobab tree, with branches as thick as most trees' trunks, and the aromatic ylang-ylang tree, whose blossoms yield an essential oil used in Chanel No. 5 perfume. In the Window to the Tropics conservatory, 16,000sq ft (1,500sq m) of exhibits and displays explore the complex and threatened ecology of the world's rainforests, providing stark evidence of the ongoing destruction. The gardens' 1939 gatehouse, constructed from local coral rock, is a museum of plant exploration.

Escape the bustle of Miami at Matheson Hammock Park

Matheson Hammock Park

A wonderful slice of natural southern Florida, Matheson Hammock Park comprises many acres of trees and coastal vegetation linked by shady pathways and culminating in a stretch of sand that, in 1930, became Miami's first public beach.

Escape This is definitely a low-key highlight with a family feel, a day at the beach that provides a welcome respite from Miami's high-octane razzmatazz, and is easily combined with another South Miami attraction. The 100-acre (40ha) park borders the Fairchild Tropical Botanic Garden, off Old Cutler Road, the old slow and scenic route south along the bay. A popular escape with the locals on the weekend, the park is very quiet during the week and a great place for families to picnic and splash about in the ocean. The shallow and wave-free man-made Atoll Pool, fringed by palm trees and flushed out daily by the tide, is a bonus for little kids bowled over by the Atlantic waves. Away from the small sandy beach, there are nature trails and bike paths criss-crossing the park, mangrove-fringed wetland areas with good birding and crab-hunting, a campsite and canoe launch. Fishermen can buy bait and tackle from the dockmaster, and the Red Fish Grill restaurant in a historic coral rock building is an alternative to the barbecue grill and is open into the evening.

On the water At the heart of the park is the sheltered Matheson Hammock Marina, home to the Castle Harbor Sailing School (▷ Tip).

THE BASICS

✚ Off map to south
✉ 9610 Old Cutler Road, South Coral Gables
☎ 305/665-5475
🕐 Dawn–dusk
🍴 Restaurant and café; both closed Mon
🚌 65
♿ Few
💲 Inexpensive

HIGHLIGHTS

● Atoll Pool
● Dinghy sailing
● Wetlands trails
● Catching crabs in the tidal pond

TIP

● Castle Harbor Sailing School (tel 305/668-8388, www.castleharbor.com) offers sailboat and power-boat rentals and tuition, dinghy lessons and two-day Learn to Sail courses, as well as race and perform-ance clinics for more experienced sailors.

Miami Metrozoo

HIGHLIGHTS

● Komodo dragons
● Bengal tigers
● Koalas
● Himalayan black bear
● Giraffe Feeding Station

TIPS

● You can buy tickets online and print them out to save time and money.
● Families with small children should consider renting a safari cycle at the entrance. Small cycles take three adults and two children; large ones six adults and two children.

Spread across almost 300 cageless acres (117ha), Miami Metrozoo offers the chance to see white tigers, Komodo dragons, koalas, crocodiles, elephants and many more creatures from around the world.

Special creatures With fewer than 100 believed to be in existence and none remaining in the wild, the zoo's prowling white Bengal tigers, with their pale fur and blue eyes, make a spectacular beginning to your zoo visit. No less memorable are the cuddly koalas, the long black tongues of the feeding giraffes, and the impressive Komodo dragons, natives of Indonesia and the largest and most powerful species of lizard on the planet. In total, the zoo is home to around 1,300 creatures with more than 80 exhibits arranged along a

Clockwise from left: a Komodo dragon, the largest lizard on the planet; a white tiger takes a break in the sun...and poses on the grass; the zoo's Asian River Life section

3-mile (5km) winding trail through grounds landscaped with beautiful flowering trees and plants.

Totally tropical Metrozoo's exhibits are grouped geographically and the newest phase, Tropical America, is scheduled to open in late 2008. At 27 acres (11ha), this showcase for animals from South America's tropical zone is bigger than the average American zoo. It will feature giant river otters, jaguars, anacondas and harpy eagles among its keynote exhibits. Regular, informative presentations on the animals take place at the amphitheater and the zoo keepers are happy to answer questions. A 2-mile (3km) monorail ride and zoo tram make sporadic circuits of the site, but strollers are essential for tackling the distances with small children in tow, or rent a safari cycle (▷ Tips).

THE BASICS

www.miamimetrozoo.com
✚ Off map to southwest
✉ 12400 SW 152nd Street (0.5 miles/0.8km west of the Florida Turnpike)
☎ 305/251-0400
🕐 Daily 9.30–5.30; last entry 4pm
🍴 Fast-food areas
🚌 Zoo Express, from Dadeland North
♿ Good
💲 Expensive

More to See

ANCIENT SPANISH MONASTERY

This 12th-century Spanish monastery from Segovia in Spain was imported to the US by William Randolph Hearst in 1925. The crates were impounded on the New York dock, to be resold in 1952 to two Miami entrepreneurs. They did their best to reconstruct the building as a tourist attraction, but progress was slow as the pieces had been incorrectly repacked in New York. The finished article is charming, but slightly higgledy-piggledy, with several modern enhancements, such as the Cuban-tiled floor. The monastery re-acquired a religious function in 1964, when the Episcopal Church bought it.

✚ Off map to north ✉ 16711 W Dixie Highway, North Miami Beach ☎ 305/945-1462 ◷ Mon–Sat 9–4, Sun 12–4 🚌 3, E, H, V ♿ Good 💲 Inexpensive

COOPERTOWN AIRBOAT RIDES

Everglades airboat rides are a thorny subject in some circles. Unscrupulous operators do cause damage to the environment and some noise pollution is inevitable. That said, Coopertown has been in business since 1945 and its airboats have access to areas in the Everglades National Park (▷ 104). Their 45-minute excursions are fun and informative, and include visits to a hardwood hammock.

✚ Off map to west ✉ 22700 SW 8th Street, US41/ Tamiami Trail (11 miles/18km west of Florida Turnpike) ☎ 305/226-6048 ◷ Daily 🍴 Restaurant ♿ Few 💲 Expensive

CORAL CASTLE

Jilted by his 16-year-old fiancée, broken-hearted Ed Leedskalnin left Latvia for North America, settling in southern Florida in around 1920. He began quarrying coral rock, over 1,100 tons in all, and sculpted the huge blocks into outsize pieces of furniture with which to decorate his Coral Castle, presumed to be a memorial to his unrequited love. The sculptures include a 9-ton gate, so well balanced that it can be opened by finger pressure; the 1,000-lb (455kg) rock chairs that gently pivot back and forth; and the Florida Table, its shape and

The cloisters of the Ancient Spanish Monastery

Coral Castle's basic kitchen

dimensions exactly proportionate to those of the state. How Leedskalnin, who died in 1951, managed this feat using only hand tools is a mystery.

➕ Off map to southwest ✉ 28655 S Dixie Highway, Homestead ☎ 305/248-6345 🕐 Sun–Thu 8–6, Fri, Sat 8–9 🚌 35, 70 ♿ Few 💲 Moderate

DEERING ESTATE AT CUTLER

Charles Deering's waterfront preserve (360 acres/144ha) on Biscayne Bay could not be more different from his brother James's manicured Vizcaya estate (▷ 82–83). The grounds are now a country park with coastal mangrove areas, pinelands, palms and tropical hardwood hammocks, as well as a Tequesta Indian burial mound and fossil pits. You can tour the grounds on foot or reserve a place on the excellent guided canoe trip. Deering's stone mansion and a timber-framed hotel are being restored and are open to visitors. Don't miss the ranger-led tours.

➕ Off map to south ✉ 16701 SW 72nd Avenue ☎ 305/235-1668 🕐 Daily 10–5 ♿ Few 💲 Moderate

GOLD COAST RAILROAD MUSEUM

The Gold Coast Railroad Museum, near Miami Metrozoo, displays relics from the halcyon days of US rail travel, including the only custom-built Presidential Pullman car. There are train rides on weekends.

➕ Off map to southwest ✉ 12450 SW 152nd Street, South Miami ☎ 305/253-0063 🕐 Daily 11–4 🚌 Zoo Express, from Dadeland North ♿ Good 💲 Inexpensive

MONKEY JUNGLE

Much is made of Monkey Jungle's free-ranging macaque colony, whose members roam the subtropical woodlands unrestricted by cages, while the humans watching them are confined to fenced-in walkways. Most of the other inhabitants lead a more restricted existence in conventional caged habitats. Additional attractions include shows, parrots and a large collection of southern Florida fossils.

➕ Off map to southwest ✉ 14805 SW 216th Street ☎ 305/235-1611 🕐 Daily 9.30–5 🍴 Snack bar ♿ Few 💲 Expensive

Visit the Monkey Jungle to see a fascinating variety of monkeys

Excursions

EXCURSIONS

FARTHER AFIELD

102

THE BASICS

www.floridakeys.org
Distance: 160 miles
(257km) from Miami to Key
West; 110 miles (177km)
from Key Largo to Key West
🛈 Florida Keys Visitor
Center, 106000 Overseas
Highway/US1 (MM 106), Key
Largo, tel 305/451-4747 or
1-800/822-1088; daily 9–6
❓ The route down the
Keys on the Overseas
Highway (US1) begins just
south of Florida City at Mile
Marker (MM) 126, and con-
tinues south to Key West at
MM 0. Mile Markers help
drivers locate attractions.
Some sections of the drive
are single lane in each
direction, and speed limits
(maximum 50mph/80kph)
are rigorously enforced. It is
best to set aside a whole day
to make the trip, with stops
along the way. Traffic on
weekends and holidays can
be a bumper-to-bumper
nightmare

HIGHLIGHTS

● John Pennekamp Coral
Reef State Park, MM 102.5
● Crane Point Hammock
Museum, MM 50.5
● Seven Mile Bridge, MM 47
● A swim at Bahia Honda
State Park, MM 37
● Key West, MM 0
● Duval Street, Key West

THE FLORIDA KEYS

**An hour's drive south of Miami, the
Florida Keys angle off the peninsula in a
spectacular chain of islands set in shim-
mering blue-green seas. From the city,
you can visit the northernmost Keys on a
day trip, but it's best to plan a leisurely
excursion with a stay in funky Key West.**

The Upper Keys Key Largo is the largest of the
42 islands and gateway to the undersea delights
of the John Pennekamp Coral Reef State Park
(MM 102.5). This is a major attraction for divers
and snorkelers, and you can also take trips out in
a glass-bottomed boat. Heading south is the sport-
fishing center of Islamorada, which is also home
to the Theater of the Sea marine park (MM 84.5).

The Middle and Lower Keys From north to
south, Grassy Key has the Dolphin Research
Center (MM 59), while capital Marathon has a
restored railroad workers' camp and the family-
friendly museums at Crane Point Hammock (MM
50.5). The magnificent Seven Mile Bridge (MM
47) marks the transition from the Middle to the
Lower Keys. Just south of it is Bahia Honda State
Park (MM 37); and the National Key Deer Refuge
offers a haven for this small and endangered
species. The end of the line is fun-loving Key
West, the southernmost point in the continental
US. The heart of downtown is mile-long Duval
Street, packed full of boutiques and bars. Around
town, shipwreck museums, family attractions and
historic buildings vie for attention. Don't miss
sunset at Mallory Square—the ultimate Key
West experience.

Pirates Pirates once overran this isolated and
treacherous maze of reefs and keys. Tourism arrived
with Henry Flagler's "railroad that went to the sea"
in 1912. The railroad was destroyed by a hurricane
in 1935 and replaced by the Overseas Highway
(US1), named for the 43 bridges that link the island
chain from Key Largo to Key West.

Distance: 45 miles (72km) from central Miami to the Ernest F. Coe Visitor Center via the Florida Turnpike and US1 (10 miles/16km west of Florida City on SR 9336); 38 miles (60km) from the Visitor Center to Flamingo (SR 9336) on the Gulf coast; 17 miles (27km) from Florida Turnpike to Shark Valley Entrance via US41/Tamiami Trail

🛈 Ernest F. Coe Visitor Center, tel 305/242-7700; Nov–end Apr daily 8–5; May–end Oct daily 9–5

🍴 Bring drinks or snacks as there are no cafés

♿ Few

💵 Moderate

Shark Valley

☎ 305/221-8776

🕐 Nov–end Apr daily 8–5; May–end Oct daily 9–5

♿ Few

💵 Moderate

❓ Tram tours during winter (reservations advisable); reduced service in summer

---

HIGHLIGHTS

● Anhinga Trail (off SR 9336) for alligator-spotting
● Gumbo Limbo Trail (off SR 9336) to experience jungley tropical woodlands
● Coopertown Airboat Rides (▷ 100)
● Shark Valley Tram Tour

THE EVERGLADES

A vast "river of grass" that once flowed south from Lake Okeechobee to the Gulf of Mexico, the Everglades is as synonymous with Florida as South Beach and Disney. Though its boundaries have been drawing in for decades, these secretive wetlands still cover more than a million acres (404,000ha) and shelter a treasury of native plant and animal life.

Protected The southern portion of the Everglades has been protected as a National Park since 1947. The main entrance lies south of Miami, near Florida City, where the Ernest F. Coe Visitor Center is a good place to start and pick up information about what to see and do in the park. Brochures indicate stops along the 38-mile (61km) road to Flamingo, where short boardwalk trails dive off into the sawgrass to illustrate various native habitats such as pine and hardwood hammocks (raised islands in the swamp where trees can grow). At the Royal Palm Visitor Center, the Anhinga Trail offers visitors a good chance of spotting alligators, turtles and the namesake anhinga, a long-necked diving bird. There are canoe rentals and guided boat trips from Flamingo.

Tamiami trail An alternative gateway to the park is the Shark Valley Entrance, on the cross-state Tamiami Trail (SW 8th Street) west of Downtown. Here, there is a 15-mile (24km) loop road with an observation tower; bicycle rentals are available. However, the best way to see around is on an informative two-hour guided tram tour and you'll get to see lots of wildlife through the trained eyes of a ranger.

When to go The winter dry season (Nov–Apr) is the best time to visit, when animals and birds congregate around waterholes. There is less to see in summer and you are likely to be plagued by mosquitoes. Cover up to avoid insect bites and sunburn year-round, and bring mosquito repellent.

Shopping

AVENTURA MALL
This indoor shopping mall has a vast Nordstrom store, Bloomingdales, Macy's, Sears and JCPenney among more than 250 retail outlets, restaurants, a cinema and children's play area.
🚫 Off map ✉ 19501 Biscayne Boulevard, North Miami ☎ 305/935-1110
🚌 3, 9, E, S

DADELAND MALL
A mall of mind-boggling size, this is home to immense branches of Macy's, Saks Fifth Avenue and JCPenney, plus almost 200 specialty shops and restaurants.
🚫 Off map ✉ 7535 N Kendall Drive, Kendall ☎ 305/665-6226 🚇 Dadeland South
🚌 1, 52, 73, 87, 88

DOLPHIN MALL
Out past the airport, this sprawling retail and entertainment complex has more than 240 shops, including a Polo Ralph Lauren Factory Store and and a Tommy Hilfiger clearance outlet.
🚫 Off map ✉ 11401 NW 12th Street (at the Florida Turnpike Exit 27) ☎ 305/365-7446 🍴 Cafés/restaurants
🚌 Shuttle buses from Downtown and the airport

THE FALLS SHOPPING CENTER
This outdoor mall, which meanders around streams, fountains, lakes and waterfalls, is home to 100-plus stores.
🚫 Off map ✉ US1 at SW 136th Street, Kendall area
☎ 305/255-4570 🚌 52, 57

LOEHMANNS'S FASHION ISLAND
Overshadowed these days by the huge Aventura Mall, this work-manlike conglomeration of shops and restaurants has a massive branch of Barnes & Noble booksellers and a Publix supermarket. There's also a 16-screen cinema.
🚫 Off map ✉ 18711 NE Biscayne Boulevard (at 187th Street), North Miami
☎ 305/932-0520 🚌 3, 9

MALL OF THE AMERICAS
Some of the most dependable names in retailing, such as TJ Maxx and Home Depot, are represented in this size-able mall where virtually every shop offers lower-than-normal prices.
🚫 Off map ✉ 7795 W Flagler Street (at the Palmette Expressway/SR826)
☎ 305/261-8772 🚌 7, 11, 87

FACTORY OUTLETS
For factory outlet bargains, head south of Miami to Prime Outlets at Florida City, 250 E Palm Drive (Florida Turnpike and US1), where you will find 50 brand-name outlets, including a Nike Factory Store, Levi's Outlet by Designs and OshKosh B'Gosh (🕐 Mon–Sat 10–9, Sun 11–7).

MIAMI INTERNATIONAL MALL
Macy's, Sears and JCPenney are among the department stores here, along with 140 specialty shops, a food court and a cinema complex, close to the Florida Turnpike.
🚫 Off map ✉ 1455 N W 107th Avenue, Doral
☎ 305/593-1775 🚌 7, 41, 71

OPA-LOCKA/HIALEAH FLEA MARKET
An immense flea market in North Miami with over 1,000 stalls.
🚫 Off map ✉ 12705 N W 42nd Avenue, Hialeah
☎ 305/688-8080 🚌 42

SAWGRASS MILLS
Miamians do not flinch at the hour-long drive to Florida's largest retail and entertainment complex, housing 350 stores west of Fort Lauderdale.
🚫 Off map ✉ 12801 W Sunrise Boulevard (at Flamingo Road), Sunrise
☎ 954/846-2300

SHOPS AT SUNSET PALACE
Open-air, three-level shopping area with big-name stores, smaller ones like FAO Schwarz and wacky furniture-seller Z-Gallerie, plus a 24-screen cinema, GameWorks and IMAX theater. It's also the local nightlife hot spot.
🚫 Off map ✉ 5701 Sunset Drive (US1 at Red Road/57th Avenue), South Miami
☎ 305/663-0482 🚇 South Miami 🚌 37, 57, 72

Entertainment and Nightlife

BROADWAY BAR AND LOUNGE

An NY loft-style club with a stage for live bands and DJs spinning hip-hop, house, industrial, Latin and World music to an appreciative crowd. ☎ Off map ✉ 17813 Biscayne Boulevard, Aventura/ North Miami Beach ☎ 305/931-1900 🚍 3, V

MARTINI BAR

Live music and DJ sounds stir up the crowd at this popular SoMi version of a SoBe club. The action starts earlier than in SoBe and the drinks are a whole lot cheaper (Happy Hour until 9pm). ☎ Off map ✉ 5701 Sunset Drive (Shops at Sunset Place), South Miami ☎ 305/665-3052 🚇 South Miami 🚍 37, 57, 72

SLOPPY JOE'S

Not the Hemmingway bar of legend (that's Captain Tony's around the corner), but a jam-packed saloon, with live rock and blues nightly from 10pm. You could just drop by for one of the excellent frozen cocktails.

☎ Off map ✉ 201 Duval Street, Key West ☎ 305/294-5717

VIRGILIO'S

There's great live music— jazz, Cuban, Latin—at this martini-fueled nightspot behind La Trattoria Italian restaurant. Try a classy gin-based martini with a twist, or tempt fate with Russian vanilla vodka or other exotic offerings. Late-night dancing in a garden setting. ☎ Off map ✉ 524 Duval Street, Key West ☎ 305/296-8118

Restaurants

PRICES

Prices are approximate, based on a three-course meal for one person.
$$$ over $40
$$ $20–$40
$ under $20

BLUE HEAVEN ($$)

In the Bahama Village district, this funky old wooden house has outdoor trestles and free-range chickens foraging under your feet. Terrific food includes fruity breakfast pancakes and divine yellowtail snapper in a citron beurre blanc. ☎ Off map ✉ 729 Thomas Street (at Petronia Street), Key West ☎ 305/296-8666

CRACK'D CONCH ($$)

This dockside shack has a reputation for superb fresh seafood. Don't expect much in the way of frills and fine linen, but enjoy the garlicky calamari, the scrumptious crabcakes and the fish of the day. If you haven't tried a conch fritter, this is a good place to start. You may also find gator nuggets on the menu. ☎ Off map ✉ Overseas Highway at MM 105, Key Largo ☎ 305/451-0732 ⊘ Closed Tue, Wed

WHO ATE ALL THE PIE?

Fans of Key lime pie should head for a café called Key Lime Pie Heaven, at 310 Front Street, Key West. One slice of the rich, tangy, oozy, meringue-topped wonder food from this place and you will be on-side with the angels. Heaven-to-go, or you can settle in with a cup of coffee at the café upstairs.

EL TORO TACO ($)

A useful stop en route to the Keys or after visiting the Everglades National Park. Generous servings of Mexican food, from the well-stuffed taco shells to piping hot (but not-too-spicy) fajitas. ☎ Off map ✉ 1 Krome Avenue, Homestead ☎ 305/245-8182 🚍 34, 35, 38, 70

Location is as important as price when choosing accommodations in Miami. From hostels and art deco boutique hotels in the heart of SoBe to luxury beachfront properties or a championship golfing resort, there is something to suit every taste.

Where to Stay

Introduction

Beachfront high-rise or art deco gem, accommodations in Miami come in all shapes and sizes. The city currently packs in around 43,500 guest rooms in an impressive variety of hotels, motels and spas.

Where to Stay

Miami Beach offers the greatest choice of accommodations in both style and price range. At the heart of the action is South Beach (SoBe), offering art deco hotels close to the clubs, shopping and dining, as well as some hostels. Note that proximity to the entertainment district can mean limited facilities in many properties and late-night noise can be a problem. North of SoBe on Collins Avenue, the best of the boutique hotels can be found above Lincoln Road, before "Hotel Row" and its famous 1950s MiMo (Miami Modern) landmarks, such as the Fontainebleau. The spacious resorts and condo-hotels that now line the beachfront all the way to Sunny Isles tend to provide far superior facilities to their SoBe counterparts in terms of pools, beach access and family-friendly activities. Exclusive neighborhoods such as Coral Gables and Coconut Grove also have their share of upscale accommodations, which are convenient for the airport. Downtown has several spectacular modern complexes aimed primarily at the corporate sector.

When to Go

The peak season in Miami is winter (Dec–Apr) but even in summer hotels fill up over July 4 and Labor Day weekends. Prices do rise significantly in high season and you need to reserve ahead.

A sign on the Colony Hotel; the Carlton Hotel; the Cardozo and Cavalier hotels; The Biltmore

TRAVEL ON A BUDGET

● The view can add a considerable amount to the bill: Ocean views attract premium rates.

● Many hotels and motels do not charge for children under 18 sharing a room with their parents.

● For stays of a month or more, apartments can be much better value than hotels; check out www.rentmiami.com

Budget Hotels

PRICES

Expect to pay under $100 for the hotel's lowest-priced room on a week night off season.

BEST WESTERN OCEANFRONT RESORT

www.bestwesternflorida.com
This all-suite beachfront property on Miami Beach has two pools, a restaurant and fitness center. It's close to dining, shopping and golf.
⊞ Off map ✉ 9365 Collins Avenue, Bal Harbour ☎ 305/864-2232; fax 305/864-3045
🚌 G, H, K, R, S, T

THE CLAY HOTEL AND INTERNATIONAL HOSTEL

www.clayhotel.com
Simple private rooms and small dormitories are housed in a 1920s Mediterranean-style building.
⊞ K3 ✉ 1438 Washington Avenue, Miami Beach ☎ 305/534-2988 or 800/379-2529; fax 305/673-0346
🚌 C, H, K, South Beach Local

GABLES INN

www.thegablesinn.net
Convenient for South Miami and the University campus, the Gables' eye-catching orange paintwork and Mediterranean-style architecture makes it hard to miss. The rooms are comfy.
⊞ B9 ✉ 730 S Dixie Highway, Coral Gables ☎ 305/661-7999 or 305/668-4467 🚌 48

JAZZ ON SOUTH BEACH

www.jazzhostels.com
This hostel, a block from the beach in SoFi, has dorms, private rooms, a lobby bar and terrace, free Wi-Fi, plus a club coordinator who arranges admission to top clubs for guests on escorted tours.
⊞ K5 ✉ 321 Collins Avenue, Miami Beach ☎ 305/672-2137; fax 305/672-4227
🚌 H, M, South Beach Local

MIAMI BEACH INTERNATIONAL TRAVELERS HOSTEL

Low-price dormitories and inexpensive private rooms. The hostel is well located with a spacious kitchen.
⊞ K4 ✉ 236 9th Street, Miami Beach ☎ 305/534-0268; fax 305/534-5862
🚌 C, H, K, South Beach Local

RESERVATION SERVICES

The following companies provide information on Miami accommodations and can make reservations on your behalf: Central Reservation Service (☎ 407/740-6442 or 800/555-7555; fax 407/740-8222; in UK, tel 0208 090 3446; www.crs hotels.com); Florida Sun-Break (☎ 305/ 672-9399 or 887/767-8634; fax 305/672-7778; www.florida sunbreak.com); South Beach Luxury Hotels (☎ 204/992-5202 or 888/238-0167; www.south beachluxuryhotels.com).

SOUTH BEACH PLAZA VILLAS

www.southbeachplazavillas.com
Refurbished in urban chic, the former Brigham Gardens guesthouse retains its lovely gardens full of tropical flowers, birdsong and waterfalls. It offers small but comfy bungalows and rooms, in a great SoBe location.
⊞ K3 ✉ 1411 Collins Avenue, Miami Beach ☎ 305/531-1331; fax 305/534-0341 🚌 C, H, K, M, S, South Beach Local

THUNDERBIRD RESORT MIAMI

www.thunderbirdresortmiami.com
This basic, family-friendly beachfront option has 180 rooms, a pool and a coffee shop. It's close to restaurants and super-markets and there's a free shuttle to Aventura Mall, Bal Harbour Shops and South Beach.
⊞ Off map ✉ 18401 Collins Avenue, Sunny Isles ☎ 305/931-7700; fax 305/932-7521 🚌 E, K, S, V

THE TROPICS HOTEL AND HOSTEL

www.tropicshotel.com
A terrific SoBe bargain a minute from the beach in a renovated art deco building. There are simple, clean rooms, dormitories, a pool, kitchen and laundry.
⊞ K3 ✉ 1550 Collins Avenue, Miami Beach ☎ 305/531-0361; fax 305/531-8676 🚌 C, H, K, M, S, South Beach Local

Mid-Range Hotels

THE ALBION

www.rubellhotels.com
A nautical deco (blues and greens prevail) hotel with a fancy pool and 96 simple, stylish rooms.
⊞ K2 ✉ 1650 James Avenue, Miami Beach ☎ 305/913-1000 or 877/RUBELLS; fax 305/531-4580 ⊟ C, G, H, K, L, M, S, South Beach Local

AVALON & MAJESTIC

www.southbeachhotels.com
Art deco hotel with 105 unelaborate but comfortable rooms. Fun bar and a good restaurant.
⊞ K4 ✉ 700 Ocean Drive, Miami Beach ☎ 305/538-0133 or 800/933-3306; fax 305/534-0258 ⊟ C, H, K, South Beach Local

CARDOZO HOTEL

www.cardozohotel.com
A Streamline Moderne classic restored by Gloria Estefan. The 43 rooms have a contemporary look. There's a bar and terrace restaurant.
⊞ K3 ✉ 1300 Ocean Drive, Miami Beach ☎ 305/535-6500 or 800/782-6500; fax 305/532-3563 ⊟ C, G, H, K, L, M, S, South Beach Local

CATALINA HOTEL AND BEACH CLUB

www.catalinahotel.com
The Catalina is a fun base for party animals and is spread over two buildings, one with a funky-kitschy lobby, the other with a bar, pool table and sidewalk café. They share a small pool, sundeck and Zen garden, close to the beach and Lincoln Road.
⊞ K2 ✉ 1732 Collins Avenue, Miami Beach ☎ 305/674-1160; fax 305/674-7522 ⊟ C, G, H, K, L, M, S, South Beach Local

DAVID WILLIAM

www.davidwilliamhotel.com
Popular with business travelers, the 34 rooms/suites are spacious and comfortable. There's a rooftop pool, restaurant and shuttle to Biltmore's recreation facilities.
⊞ B6 ✉ 700 Biltmore Way, Coral Gables ☎ 305/445-7821 or 800/757-8073; fax 305/913-1933 ⊟ 24, 42, 56, J

DOUBLETREE

www.coconutgrove.doubletree.com
A modern high-rise in the heart of Coconut Grove.

Some of the 196 rooms have fantastic bay views.
⊞ D8 ✉ 2649 S Bayshore Drive, Coconut Grove ☎ 305/858-2500 or 800/222-8733; fax 305/858-9117 ⊟ Coconut Grove ⊟ 48, 249

ESSEX HOUSE

www.essexhotel.com
A 1930s Moderne hotel tastefully restored with art deco furnishings and 74 relaxing rooms, as well as suites, a tropical courtyard and a lounge bar.
⊞ K4 ✉ 1001 Collins Avenue ☎ 305/673-6595 or 800/553-7739; fax 305/673-6530 ⊟ C, H, K, W

HAMPTON INN

www.hamptoninncoconutgrove.com
This comfortable chain hotel with a pool makes a good touring base and offers free breakfast, local calls, parking and internet access.
⊞ D7 ✉ 2800 SW 28th Terrace, Coconut Grove ☎ 305/448-2800 or 800/426-7866; fax 305/442-8655 ⊟ Coconut Grove ⊟ 40, 56, J

HOTEL ST. MICHEL

Art nouveau finds a Miami showcase in this 1926 hotel with 27 individually furnished rooms and a warm, romantic atmosphere. Highly regarded restaurant.
⊞ C6 ✉ 162 Alcazar Avenue, Coral Gables ☎ 305/444-1666 or 800/848-4683; fax 305/529-0074 ⊟ 24, 42, 56, J

INDIAN CREEK HOTEL

www.indiancreekhotel.com
Inviting, restored art deco
property with 61 rooms
on a quiet street a short
walk from the heart of
South Beach. Art deco
furnishings and a fine
restaurant with some out-
door seating, plus a pool.
🔲 Off map 🖂 2727 Indian
Creek Drive ☎ 305/531-2727
or 800/491-2772; fax 305/531-
5651 🚌 C, M, G, H, L, S

INTERCONTINENTAL MIAMI

www.icmiamihotel.com
The 640 guestrooms
here are comfortable,
well-equipped and offer
fabulous views across the
Port of Miami and
Biscayne Bay from the
Downtown waterfront.
Restaurants, bars, pool.
🔲 F4 🖂 100 Chopin Plaza,
Miami ☎ 305/577-1000 or
800/327-3005; fax 305/372-
4440 🅿 Bayfront Park
🚌 3, 11, 16, 77, C, S

MIAMI INTERNATIONAL AIRPORT HOTEL

www.miahotel.com
The only on-site airport
hotel has a restaurant
overlooking the runways
and soundproofed rooms.
Alternatively, there are
chain hotels (Days Inn,
Hampton, Marriott)
nearby offering 24-hour
airport shuttles.
🔲 Off map 🖂 Miami
International Airport
☎ 305/871-4100 or 800/327-
1276; fax 305/871-0800
🚌 All serving MIA

PARK CENTRAL HOTEL

www.theparkcentral.com
This art deco hotel has
been restored in 1940s
style, with 125 rooms,
dining and fine views to
the ocean.
🔲 K4 🖂 640 Ocean Drive,
Miami Beach ☎ 305/538-
1611 or 800/727-5236; fax
305/534-7520 🚌 C, H, K,
South Beach Local

PELICAN HOTEL

www.pelicanhotel.com
You can stay here for
less, but the money-no-
object guest can spend
up to $2,500 a night on
one of the 30 theme
rooms (▷ panel).
🔲 K4 🖂 826 Ocean Drive,
Miami Beach ☎ 305/673-
3373 or 800/773-5422; fax
305/673-3255 🚌 C, H,
K, South Beach Local

SONESTA HOTEL AND SUITES

www.sonesta.com/
coconutgrove
Sonesta has 215 rooms
and one- and two-bed-
room suites, most with

FANTASTIC DECOR

South Beach is full of some
stunning designer-led hotels,
but there's nothing to
compare with guestrooms at
the Pelican (▷ this page).
The designers have gone all
out to entertain guests'
wildest fantasies, from the
industrial muscle of With
Drill to the western-style
High Corral, OK Chaparral.

balconies with bay views.
Rooftop pool, dining, bar.
🔲 D8 🖂 2889 McFarlane
Road, Coconut Grove ☎ 305/
529-2828 or 800/SONESTA; fax
305/529-2008 🚌 48, 249

STANDARD

www.standardhotel.com
Anything but standard,
this 105-room hotel-with-
spa makes a virtue of its
off-SoBe location on quiet
Belle Isle. Utterly relaxing
(lots of hydrotherapy,
yoga, Turkish baths), but
only minutes away from
the beach and Lincoln
Road. Restaurant and bar.
🔲 H2 🖂 40 Island Avenue,
Miami Beach ☎ 305/673-
1717; fax 305/673-8181 🚌 A

TOWNHOUSE

www.townhousehotel.com
Welcoming boutique
hotel with 107 compact
but comfy rooms, and a
funky rooftop deck with
waterbeds. The breakfast
is Parisian, sushi is served
in the lounge.
🔲 L2 🖂 150 20th Street,
Miami Beach ☎ 305/534-
3800 or 877/534-3800; fax
305/534-3811 🚌 C, G, H, L,
M, S

WALDORF TOWERS

www.waldorftowers.com
An art deco landmark in
the heart of SoBe, with
45 compact and function-
al rooms. Those at the
front have ocean views.
🔲 K4 🖂 860 Ocean Drive,
Miami Beach ☎ 305/531-
7684 or 800/933-2322; fax
305/672-6836 🚌 C, H, K,
South Beach Local

WHERE TO STAY MID-RANGE HOTELS

Luxury Hotels

WHERE TO STAY LUXURY HOTELS

PRICES

Expect to pay more than $250 for the hotel's lowest-priced room on a week night off season.

THE BILTMORE
See page 64.

THE DELANO
www.delano-hotel.com
One of Miami's most fashionable hotels, with all-white interiors by Philippe Starck and a celebrity clientele.
➕ J2 ✉ 1685 Collins Avenue ☎ 305/672-2000 or 800/555-5001; fax 305/532-0099 🚍 C, G, M, H, L, S

DORAL GOLF RESORT AND SPA
www.doralresort.com
This top US golf resort has five championship courses, 693 luxurious rooms and suites, fine dining, European-style spa facilities and the Blue Lagoon pool.
➕ Off map ✉ 4400 NW 87th Avenue, Doral ☎ 305/592-2000 or 800/713-6725; fax 305/594-4682 🚍 87

FONTAINEBLEAU MIAMI BEACH
www.fontainbleau.com
Most of the guest rooms, though comfortable, are less impressive than the design and spacious grounds of this landmark building (▷ 51).
➕ Off map ✉ 4441 Collins Avenue, Miami Beach ☎ 305/538-2000 or 800/548-8886; fax 305/673-5351 🚍 G, H, J, L, S, T

LOEWS MIAMI BEACH
www.loewshotels.com
This giant hotel borders SoBe with sumptuously landscaped grounds, staircases decorated with palm trees and 800 luxurious rooms (and butler-staffed beach cabanas).
➕ K/L2 ✉ 1601 Collins Avenue ☎ 305/604-1601; fax 305/604-1601 🚍 C, G, H, M, S

THE RALEIGH
www.raleighhotel.com
A renovated 1940s landmark with 105 rooms, every conceivable facility, a stunning pool and a guest list of glitterati.
➕ L2 ✉ 1775 Collins Avenue, Miami Beach ☎ 305/ 534-6300 or 800/848-1775; fax 305/538-8140 🚍 C, M, G, H, L, S

THE SAGAMORE
www.sagamorehotel.com
Fabulous modern art is the defining theme of this

BATHING BELLES

Miami isn't short of a swimming pool or two, but there are a couple that really stand out from the crowd. The vast colonnaded swimming pool at the Biltmore is one of the wonders of the "City Beautiful." It currently contains some 600,000 gallons of water, half its original capacity! And for sublime elegance, the sculpted contours of the palm-fringed pool at The Raleigh are the hotel's jewel in the crown.

upscale but determinedly low-key hotel. Spacious suites, beachfront pool and water sports.
➕ L2 ✉ 1671 Collins Avenue, Miami Beach ☎ 305/535-8088 or 877/242-6673; fax 305/535-8185 🚍 C, G, H, L, M, S, South Beach Local

THE SETAI
www.setai.com
A cool Asian-theme art deco hotel with 87 thoughtfully equipped rooms, lovely gardens, pools and a fabulous spa.
➕ L2 ✉ 2001 Collins Avenue, Miami Beach ☎ 305/ 520-6000 or 877/997-3824; fax 305/520-6111 🚍 C, G, H, L, M, S

THE SHORE CLUB
www.shoreclub.com
Über-chic minimalist design makes the perfect setting for beautiful people to swan around. The Skybar is one of the hottest nightspots on the beach.
➕ L2 ✉ 1901 Collins Avenue, Miami Beach ☎ 305/695-3100 or 877/640-9500 🚍 C, G, H, L, M, S

TRUMP INTERNA-TIONAL SONESTA BEACH RESORT
www.trumpsonesta.com
A family-friendly place with 390 rooms and suites with views, a spa, pools, water sports and kids' activities. Suites have a kitchen and washer/drier.
➕ Off map ✉ 18001 Collins Avenue, Sunny Isles Beach ☎ 305/692-5600 or 800/766-3782; fax 305/692-5601 🚍 G, H, S, T

This section will help you plan for your trip to Miami, and provide you with the information you'll need on arrival, as well as details of how to get around the city and other essential facts.

Need to Know

Planning Ahead

When to Go

December to April are Miami's busiest months, when the weather is sunny and warm. Peak periods are over Christmas and New Year's Eve, and the March–April Spring Break. It is quieter in late spring or fall. Despite summer's high humidity and thunderstorms, events continue all year.

TIME

Miami is on Eastern Standard Time, 3 hours ahead of the West Coast, 5 hours behind GMT.

AVERAGE DAILY MAXIMUM TEMPERATURES											
JAN	FEB	MAR	APR	MAY	JUN	JUL	AUG	SEP	OCT	NOV	DEC
67°F	68°F	72°F	74°F	79°F	81°F	83°F	83°F	82°F	78°F	72°F	69°F
19°C	20°C	22°C	24°C	26°C	27°C	28°C	28°C	27°C	26°C	23°C	21°C

Spring brings a gentle increase in temperature, which makes the ocean more inviting. Humidity increases, too.

Summer is when humidity is highest, and there are frequent short, sharp thunderstorms, generally in the afternoon. Hurricane season begins in June; the vast majority of hurricanes bypass the city.

Fall sees humidity start to drop, though hurricane season officially lasts until November.

Winter is warm and sunny, with low humidity.

WHAT'S ON

January *Orange Bowl*: Culmination of the college football season.

Art Deco Weekend: Walks, tours and other events celebrate South Beach's architecture.

February *Miami Film Festival*: Celebration of independent films, most from North, Central and South America.

March *Calle Ocho Festival*: Little Havana's lively celebration of Cuban culture, with floats, food stands and dancing.

June *Goombay Festival*: Caribbean music, food and much more in Coconut Grove's Peacock Park.

July *America's Birthday Bash*: Bayfront Park is the focus of the city's Independence Day party.

August *Miami Spice Restaurant Month*: Eateries all over the city offer a special fixed-price menu.

September *Festival Miami*: Performing arts events at the University of Miami (continues into November).

October *Columbus Day Regatta*: A small armada of yachts races out of Key Biscayne.

November *Miami Book Fair*: Major event for international publishers and authors; open to the public.

The White Party: A week-long gay fundraiser for HIV/AIDS charities held around the Thanksgiving weekend, culminating in a gala dinner at Vizcaya.

December *Art Basel Miami Beach/Design Miami*: Prestigious international art and design fairs run concurrently in Miami Beach and the Design District.

Miami Online

www.miamiandbeaches.com

The site of the Greater Miami Convention and Visitors Bureau offers a wealth of information. Check out maps, attractions, upcoming events, shopping and special offer information. You can also make hotel and restaurant reservations.

www.miamidesigndistrict.net

Check out the latest news on events in the Miami Design District. There are showroom listings, restaurant and club information, and web-cam visuals depicting sunny sidewalks, arresting architecture and beautiful people.

www.mdpl.com

The Miami Design Preservation League is the force behind the rejuvenation of the Miami Beach art deco district. Their website contains historical information, details of guided walking tours and a calendar of events.

www.southbeach-usa.com

News, reviews, gossip and more from the hottest spot on Miami Beach. Find out who's been living it up in SoBe, catch up on the best nightspots and view the glamorous photos.

www.miamiherald.com

Miami's leading daily newspaper provides balanced coverage of local, statewide and Latin-American news online. The Friday edition carries a useful Weekend section with details of theater, film, music and dance events in the city for the week ahead, plus restaurant listings.

www.GoGayMiami.com

Primarily a business-oriented organization, the Miami-Dade Gay and Lesbian Chamber of Commerce website also lists events and club happenings of interest to the gay community.

www.miamidade.gov/parks

A useful site for checking out facilities, activities and events in Miami's many outdoor spaces.

HOT TICKETS

If you're planning on catching NBA basketball stars the Miami Heat, the footballing Miami Dolphins or baseball-playing Florida Marlins in action during your stay, you should secure tickets in advance to avoid disappointment. Tickets to most of the city's top sporting and cultural events can be booked through TicketMaster (www.ticketmaster.com).

CLUB ROUND-UP

Check out the latest club and gig info online with the *Miami New Times* (www.miaminewtimes.com), the city's alternative free weekly newspaper. Its comprehensive listings cover clubs, lounges and music venues throughout the city for the week ahead, as well as major upcoming concerts, theater and film news and reviews.

PLANNING AHEAD

www.fodors.com

A complete travel-planning site. You can research prices and weather; book air tickets, cars and rooms; ask questions (and get answers) from fellow travelers; and find links to other sites.

Getting There

ENTRY REQUIREMENTS

All visitors to the US (including US citizens returning to the country) require a passport or valid travel document. For stays under 90 days, most EU citizens should require only a machine-readable passport (MRP) and will need to fill in a visa waiver form and immigration form supplied by their travel company or airline. Visas are required for longer stays. Under the Western Hemisphere Travel Initiative (WHTI), there may be further changes to US entry requirements. Consult your tour operator or airline, or check for updates posted on the US government travel website www.travel.state. gov. No vaccinations are required to enter the US, unless you have come from or stopped over in countries where there are epidemics.

CUSTOMS REGULATIONS

● Duty-free allowances include 32fl oz (1 liter) alcoholic spirits or wine (no one under the age of 21 may bring alcohol into the US), 200 cigarettes or 50 cigars and up to $100-worth of gifts.
● Some medication bought over the counter abroad might be prescription only in the US and may be confiscated. Bring a doctor's certificate for essential medication.

AIRPORT

Miami International Airport (MIA) is 7 miles (11km) west of Downtown, 14 miles (22km) west of Miami Beach, and handles all international and virtually all domestic flights into the city.

8 miles (13km)
6 miles (10km)
4 miles (6.5km)

Miami International Airport

Downtown Miami

ARRIVING BY AIR

Miami International Airport (MIA) handles more than 30 million people a year, making it the 12th-busiest airport in the US. There are a variety of onward transportation options for travel into the city. One of the most convenient and cost-effective is SuperShuttle (☎ 305/871-2000; www.SuperShuttle.com), which operates a fleet of blue-and-yellow minivans providing frequent services between the airport and any destination in the city. Fares are calculated according to the zip code of your destination and are prominently displayed on noticeboards (as are those of taxis) outside the baggage reclaim area. Passengers collect a shuttle boarding pass from the ticket stand and pay the driver on arrival. The journey time to Miami Beach depends on the number of people to be dropped off, but is usually around 30 minutes.

City buses also serve the airport, departing from the Metrobus stop outside Concourse E. Route J serves Miami Beach (taking 40 minutes to reach 41st Street) and, in other directions, Coral Gables (15 minutes) and Coconut Grove (30 minutes). Bus 7 links the airport with the city center (30 minutes); bus 37 with Coconut

Grove (30 minutes). Fares are $1.50, plus a small transfer fee between districts.

Taxis serve all parts of the city from the airport. The trip to Downtown takes around 20 minutes and costs around $22. Currently there are flat-rate fares for popular visitor destinations, including Miami Beach's South Beach/art deco district ($32), the Mid-Beach area ($37), Bal Harbour ($43), Sunny Isles ($52) and Key Biscayne ($41). These rates are subject to change, so check in advance (☎ 305/375-3677; www.miami-airport.com).

Many visitors choose to rent a car to explore Miami. Rental prices in Florida are some of the lowest in the US and there are numerous rental agencies at the airport. Most of the parking lots are some distance from the airport, but rental operators offer free minivan transfers from the lower concourse. Once you have finalized the paperwork, ask the clerk to mark your route on a map for you. Miami operates a "Follow the Sun" system, which marks the safer routes to popular destinations with a sunburst logo on directional signs. If you're heading for South Beach, the most direct option is SR 836 (the Dolphin Expressway), which leads directly to the art deco district via MacArthur Causeway. SR112 (Airport Expressway) goes to mid-Miami Beach via the Julia Tuttle Causeway.

ARRIVING BY BUS

Greyhound buses serve a number of locations in Miami. The main Downtown terminal is 1012 NW 1st Avenue ☎ 305/374-6160. There is also an airport stop at 4111 NW 27th Street. For information ☎ 305/871-1810 or 800/231-2222; www.greyhound.com

ARRIVING BY TRAIN

Amtrak trains terminate at 8303 NW 37th Avenue, 7 miles (11km) northwest of the city center. The station is served by bus L, which runs to Miami Beach, and is close to a MetroRail terminal, which provides access to Downtown. For information, ☎ 800/872-7245; www.amtrak.com

INSURANCE

Full travel and health insurance is strongly recommended. Check whether any existing policies offer some degree of travel cover and tailor your policy accordingly. If you have a pre-existing medical condition or you will be undertaking any form of high-risk activity, such as scuba diving, during your stay, ensure you are adequately covered.

PORT OF MIAMI

The busy Port of Miami is one of the largest cruise ports in the world. Some two million passengers pass through the facility annually and it is well-located for exploring the city. A frequent trolley service links the bayfront cruise berths with Downtown and Bayside Marketplace, and taxis are easily available.

Getting Around

SOUTH BEACH LOCAL

The best way to explore the art deco district is on foot, but you can also use the South Beach Local bus service. The circular route, which can be taken in either direction, travels north-south on Washington and West Avenues from the Convention Center on 17th Street in the north down to South Pointe. The service operates Mon–Sat 8am–1am, Sun and holidays 10am–1am, every 10–15 minutes.

There are only a few neighborhoods where exploring on foot is viable in Miami: the art deco South Beach area, Coconut Grove, the Downtown district and the Design District. Beyond these areas, transportation is essential and many people chose to drive. However, Miami-Dade County operates an extensive public transportation system, with more than 100 bus routes and the elevated single-route railroad, MetroRail. In and around Downtown, the Metromover monorail provides efficient, if slow, movement. Services become sporadic after the evening rush hour, and using public transportation at night can be dangerous, especially away from Miami Beach. For transit information contact ☎ 305/770 3131; www.miamidade.gov/transit

BIRD'S-EYE VIEW

For an overview of the Downtown district, take a ride on the Metromover. The elevated track wends its way through the skyscrapers on the inner circuit (Downtown Loop). The outer circuit (Brickell Loop) crosses the Miami River heading south to the Financial District, while the northern spur (Omni Loop) trundles past the Freedom Tower en route to the new Carnival Center for the Performing Arts.

METROBUS

● Bus services cover most areas in the city, but it is often necessary to transfer from one route to another to complete a crosstown journey.
● A flat fare of $1.50 applies; transfer to a different bus route or MetroRail within 2 hours is 50¢. The exception is the South Beach Local service, which has a flat fare of 25¢ (▷ panel).
● Pay the exact fare only into the fare box.
● To transfer to MetroRail, ask for rail transfer.
● Transfers to Metromover are free.

METROMOVER

● This free automated service circles the Downtown district, with an inner loop and an outer loop stopping at 20 stations (▷ panel).
● Connections to MetroRail can be made at Government Center and Brickell stations.
● Connections to Metrobus services can be made at the Omni and Downtown bus stations.
● A transfer fee of is $1.50 is payable for transfers to Metrobus or MetroRail.

METRORAIL

● The fare is $1.50; to transfer to a bus is 50¢.
● If required, buy a bus transfer from the machine inside the station as you enter.

PARKING

Street parking is in short supply in South Beach and Coconut Grove. Meters are available, but you will need handfuls of quarters to feed them. Parking lots are generally a better option.

● For rail journeys to South Florida destinations farther afield, you can use Tri-Rail services. Contact ☎ 800/844-7245; www.tri-rail.com.

SCHEDULES AND MAP INFORMATION
● Pick up maps showing routes and schedules from the Transit Service Centers listed above.

TAXIS
● Taxis can be hailed on the street, and are found outside major hotels and transportation termini. It is more usual to phone for one.
● Hotel receptionists, restaurant and nightclub staff will usually order a taxi on request.
● During rush hours and rain showers taxis are in heavy demand.
● Fares are $6.90 for the first mile and $2.40 for each extra mile. Waiting time is 40¢ per minute.
● If you have any complaints, ☎ 305/375-3677.
● Miami taxi firms include Flamingo ☎ 305/759-8700, Metro ☎ 305/888-8888 and Yellow ☎ 305/444-4444.

TOKENS AND CHANGE
● Tokens offer minimal savings on Metrobus and MetroRail travel (7 for $10; 10 for $14.50).
● Buy them from change machines at MetroRail stations or the Transit Service Centers on level 2 of Government Center station (✉ 111 NW 1st Street, Downtown) and level 2 of Civic Center MetroRail Station (✉ 1501 NW 12th Avenue).
● Always have the exact change ready.

VISITOR PASSES
● A 7-Day Visitor Pass allows unlimited use of Metrobus and MetroRail for $19.
● The Pass has a scratch-off panel to indicate on which dates it has been used.
● Buy it online (www.miamidade.gov/transit) or from a number of locations, including Miami International Airport (Mercado Miami, Concourse F), the Art Deco Welcome Center (✉ 1001 Ocean Drive, Miami Beach) and the Downtown Welcome Center (✉ 174 E Flagler Avenue, outside the Gusman Theater).

DRIVING IN MIAMI
Miami is fairly simple to navigate and is crisscrossed by multilane expressways that save considerable time on longer journeys.
The most important routes to fix in your mind are:
North–South
● I-95, the main north-south artery from Fort Lauderdale and the north, with a six- to eight-lane elevated section crossing Downtown.
● US-1, a slower route closer to the coast, also known as the South Dixie Highway south of Coral Gables, where it continues down to the Florida Keys.
● The Palmetto Expressway (SR 826) and the Florida Turnpike (SR 821), both inland expressways.
East–West
● The Tamiami Trail (US-41) crosses the state from Miami through the Everglades to the Gulf Coast at Naples. The eastern section through Downtown and Little Havana is known as SW 8th Street, or Calle Ocho.
● The Dolphin Expressway (SR 836) is a fast link between Downtown and the Florida Turnpike via Miami International Airport.
● Miami Beach is linked to the mainland by six well-signed causeways. The main north-south route down the barrier islands is Collins Avenue (A1A).

Essential Facts

● Fire, police or ambulance
☎ 911 (no money required).
● Rape Hotline ☎ 305/585-7273 (to report a rape);
☎ 305/585-6949 (for recovery support).
● Hospitals with emergency rooms include: Jackson Memorial Medical Center ✉ 1611 NW 12th Avenue, Downtown/Civic Center ☎ 305/585-1111; and Mt Sinai Medical Center ✉ 4300 Alton Road, Miami Beach ☎ 305/674-2121.

MONEY

The unit of currency is the dollar (100 cents). Bills (notes) come in denominations of $1, $5, $10, $20, $50 and $100; coins are 25¢ (a quarter), 10¢ (a dime), 5¢ (a nickel) and 1¢ (a penny).

5 dollars

10 dollars

50 dollars

100 dollars

ELECTRICITY
● The supply is 110 volts; 60 cycles AC current.
● US appliances use two-prong plugs. European appliances require an adapter.

LONE TRAVELERS
● Lone travelers, including women traveling alone, are not unusual in Miami.
● Women in particular may encounter unwanted attention after dark and should avoid being alone on the street except in established nightlife areas. If waiting for a cab, do so where staff of the restaurant or club you have been at can see you.

MEDICAL TREATMENT
● Hotel reception staff can assist in finding a doctor, or telephone the nonemergency Physician Referral Service ⓘ Monday–Friday 9–5 ☎ 305/324-8717.
● The Emergency Dental Referral Service (☎ 305/667-3647 or 800/336-8478) will refer you to a dentist in your area.

MEDICINES
● Pharmacies are plentiful and listed in Yellow Pages under "Drugstores." Visitors from Europe will find familiar medicines under unfamiliar names, and some drugs that are available over-the-counter at home will be issued only with a prescription.
● If you are using medication regularly, bring a supply with you (but check panel, ▷ 116, Customs Regulations). If you are intending to buy prescription drugs in the US, bring a note from your own doctor.
● There are late-night pharmacies all over the city and two branches of Walgreens that open 24-hours at ✉ 1845 Alton Road, Miami Beach ☎ 305/531-8868; and ✉ 5731 Bird Road, Coral Gables ☎ 305/666-0757.

MONEY MATTERS
● Most banks have ATMs, which accept credit cards registered in other countries that are

linked to the Cirrus or Plus networks. Ensure your PIN is valid in the US.

● Credit cards are widely accepted.

● US dollar traveler's checks function like cash in most shops; $20 and $50 denominations are most useful.

● A 6.5 percent state sales tax and local sales tax (1 percent) are added to marked retail prices; additional resort taxes (of 2–4 percent) apply to hotel accommodations and in some restaurants.

OPENING HOURS

● Shops: Monday–Saturday 9–10am to 5–6pm. Department stores, supermarkets and malls keep longer hours, as do many shops in Miami Beach and Coconut Grove.

● Sunday shopping is common.

● Bank hours: Monday–Friday 9–3, with many branches open later once a week or more and some open on Saturday 9–12.

POST OFFICES

● Post offices are generally open Monday–Friday 8.30–5, Saturday 8.30–12.30.

● Local post offices include: ⊠ 1300 Washington Avenue, Miami Beach; ⊠ 500 NW 2nd Avenue, Downtown; ⊠ 3191 Grand Avenue, Coconut Grove; and ⊠ 20 Miracle Mile (at Valencia), Coral Gables.

● For more information, contact ☎ 800/275-8777; www.usps.com.

SENSIBLE PRECAUTIONS

● Visitors should always be vigilant.

● By day, all major areas of interest to visitors are relatively safe, though it is advisable to discuss your itinerary with hotel reception staff and heed their advice.

● After dark, stick to established nightlife areas.

● Neighborhoods can change from safe to dangerous within a few blocks. Never wander idly from safe, busy streets.

● Never carry easily snatched bags and cameras, or place your wallet in your back pocket.

● When not in use, cameras and other valuables

LOST PROPERTY

● Miami International Airport ☎ 305/876-7377

● Lost on Metro-Dade Transit ☎ 305/375-3366

● Police Lost and Found ☎ 305/673-7960

TOURIST OFFICES

● Art Deco Welcome Center ⊠ 1001 Ocean Drive, Miami Beach ☎ 305/672-2014; www.mdpl.org

● Miami Beach Visitor Center ⊠ 1920 Meridian Avenue, Miami Beach ☎ 305/672-1270; www.miamibeachchamber.com

● Coconut Grove Chamber of Commerce ⊠ 2820 McFarlane Road, Coconut Grove ☎ 305/444-7270; www.coconutgrove.com

● Tropical Everglades Visitor Association ⊠ 160 Highway 1, Florida City ☎ 800/388-9669 or 305/245-9180; www.tropicaleverglades.com

● Greater Miami Convention and Visitors Bureau ⊠ 701 Brickell Avenue, Downtown ☎ 800/283-2707 or 305/539-3000; www.miamiandbeaches.com

NEED TO KNOW ESSENTIAL FACTS

NATIONAL HOLIDAYS

Jan 1 New Year's Day
Jan, 3rd Mon Martin Luther King's Birthday
Feb, 3rd Mon President's Day
May, last Mon Memorial Day
Jul 4 Independence Day
Sep, 1st Mon Labor Day
Oct, 2nd Mon Columbus Day
Nov 11 Veterans Day
Nov, 4th Thu Thanksgiving
Dec 25 Christmas Day

TELEPHONES

● Public telephones are found on the street and in public buildings. Local calls cost at least 50¢ from a pay-phone (call rates are listed in the front of the telephone directory). Insert coins before dialing (no change is given).
● Calls from hotel-room telephones are usually more expensive than from a public telephone.
● Many businesses have toll-free numbers, prefixed by 800, 866, 877 or 888. First dial '1'.

TIPPING

As a basic rule of thumb, tip at least 15 percent in a restaurant; add 15 percent to a taxi fare; allow $1 per bag for a hotel porter or airport busboy; and a small tip of $1-or-so is expected for valet parking and other minor services.

should be left in your hotel. Never carry more money than you need. Pay for major purchases with travelers' checks or credit cards.
● Replacing a stolen passport is difficult and begins with a visit or telephone call to your country's nearest consular office.
● If only in order to make an insurance claim, report stolen items to the nearest police precinct (check telephone book for addresses).

SMOKING

● Smoking is banned in all public buildings and restaurants. It is sometimes grudgingly allowed on outdoor terraces, but your neighbors may make the experience too uncomfortable to pursue.
● Miami's South American influence does mean cigar smokers can find refuge in several cigar bars and lounges.

STUDENT TRAVELERS

● An International Student Identity Card (ISIC) brings reduced admission to many museums and other attractions.
● Anyone aged under 21 is forbidden to buy alcohol and may be denied entry to some nightclubs.

VISITORS WITH DISABILITIES

● Miami, and Florida as a whole, is fairly well served with facilities for visitors with disabilities.
● Most public transportation is wheelchair accessible, including "kneeling" buses. For details, contact the Miami-Dade Transit Special Transportation Service ☎ 305/263-5400; www.miamidade.gov/transit.
● Other useful contacts include: the Miami Deaf Services Bureau ✉ 1250 NW 7th Street, Miami, FL 33125 ☎ Voice/TTY 305/560-2866; Miami Lighthouse for the Blind ✉ 601 SW 8th Avenue, Miami, FL 33130 ☎ 305/856-2288; www.miamilighthouse.com; and the Miami-Dade Office of ADA Coordination ✉ 111 NW 1st Street, Miami, FL 33128 ☎ 305/375-3566, ☎ TTY 305/375-4805; www.miamidade.gov

Language

At least half of Miami's population is Spanish-speaking. You don't need Spanish to get around, but it can be fun to learn a few words. Below are some useful Cuban-Spanish words.

MENU READER

a la brasa	braised
a la parilla	grilled
al carbon	barbecued
al horno	baked
al mojo de ajo	in butter and garlic
al vapor	steamed
agua	water
arroz	rice
asado	roasted
atún	tuna
bebida	drink
bistec	steak
bocadillo	sandwich
camarones	shrimp
cangrejo	crab
carne	meat
cerveza	beer
chorizo	spicy sausage
cocido	stew
condimentado (-a)	spicy
cordero	lamb
crudo	rare
dulce	sweet
ensalada	salad
fritas	fries or chips
frito	fried
fruta	fruit
helado	ice cream
jugo de fruta	fruit juice
langosta	lobster
leche	milk
legumbres	vegetables
mariscos	seafood
pan	bread
pescado	fish
pollo	chicken
queso	cheese
vegetariano	vegetarian
vino	wine

NUMBERS

cero	0
uno	1
dos	2
tres	3
cuatro	4
cinco	5
seis	6
siete	7
ocho	8
nueve	9
diez	10
once	11
doce	12
trece	13
catorce	14
quince	15
dieciséis	16
diecisiete	17
dieciocho	18
diecinueve	19
veinte	20
veintiuno	21
treinta	30
cuarenta	40
cincuenta	50
sesenta	60
setenta	70
ochenta	80
noventa	90
cien	100

USEFUL WORDS

sí	yes
no	no
por favor	please
gracias	thank you
hola	hello
adiós	goodbye
perdone	excuse me

Timeline

During the economically buoyant years that followed World War I, Miami boomed as thousands of northern speculators headed south to the Sunshine State, envisioning vast profits and luxurious lifestyles to be had from buying land. In the first half of the 1920s Miami's population quadrupled, and land values sometimes tripled within a day. Some developments, such as Coral Gables, were properly planned. By 1925, however, rogue agents were selling useless plots of land on a "site unseen" basis to desperate buyers. By late 1926 the boom was over, 40 city banks had closed, and a hurricane compounded the city's woes.

From left to right: A memorial commemorating the failed uprising of 1,300 Cubans attempting to overthrow Castro in 1961; the Spanish conquer the region; a statue of Alfonso at the Ancient Spanish Monastery

1513 Spaniard Juan Ponce de León makes the first European landing at the future site of Miami.

1821 After possession has switched between Spain and Britain, Florida becomes a US possession. US citizens settle predominantly in the north; in three subsequent Seminole Wars, the indigenous Seminole people are driven into the Everglades.

1843 Parcels of land in the riverside hamlet of Miami are sold for $1 each. The name "Miami" is allegedly from a Tequesta (the name given to a native tribe of the area) word meaning "sweet water."

1847 Miami's first trading post is built on the banks of the Miami River.

1860 Miami's population is 60. No roads reach the settlement, which can be accessed only by boat.

1874 The opening of a post office ensures Miami is added to official maps.

1880s Coconut Grove increases in size and renown with the arrival of the Peacock family, whose hotel becomes the area's first lodging.

1896 Standard Oil tycoon Henry Flagler extends his railroad south to Miami and opens a hotel. With its population numbering 300, Miami officially becomes a city.

1913 Entrepreneur Carl Fisher begins the dredging operation that creates Miami Beach from a coconut planation.

1921 George Merrick sells the first plot of his Coral Gables development. A land-buying frenzy grips Miami.

1926 The land boom ends in a severe slump. A devastating hurricane kills 392 people.

1934 Pan Am Airlines begins passenger flights between Miami and Latin America.

1965 The first "freedom flight" from Havana lands. Subsequent airlifts bring an estimated 230,000 Cubans to Miami.

1980 The "Mariel Boatlift" brings a further 125,000 Cubans to Miami.

1984 TV show *Miami Vice* is first broadcast.

1992 Hurricane Andrew causes $30 billion of damage.

1997 Fashion designer Gianni Versace is fatally shot outside his Ocean Drive home.

2006 The $500 million Carnival Center for the Performing Arts opens.

2007 More than 43,000 people attend December's Art Basel Miami Beach (▷ 25), making it the biggest event of its kind in the US.

ART DECO

Throughout the 1930s, hotels, theaters, apartment blocks and stores were constructed in South Beach to stimulate a tourist boom and help the local economy recover from the Depression. The 800-or-so buildings were raised in the fashionable style of the day: art deco. With porthole windows, streamlined features, bas-reliefs and tropical motifs, the buildings took on a unique look, subsequently termed tropical art deco. Launched in 1976, the Miami Design Preservation League overcame considerable opposition to have the area placed on the National Register of Historic Places in 1979, and encouraged the restoration and remodeling of the buildings.

Left to right: The Carnival Center; an art deco building on Ocean Drive; tribal chief Little Turtle, who led raids on settlers before being forced to sign the Treaty of Greenville in 1795

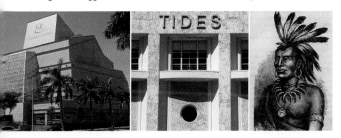

Index

INDEX

CITYPACK TOP 25
Miami

WRITTEN BY Mick Sinclair
ADDITIONAL WRITING Emma Stanford
DESIGN CONCEPT Kate Harling
COVER DESIGN AND DESIGN WORK Jacqueline Bailey
INDEXER Marie Lorimer
IMAGE RETOUCHING AND REPRO Michael Moody, Sarah Montgomery
EDITOR Kathryn Glendenning
SERIES EDITORS Paul Mitchell, Edith Summerhayes

First published 1997
Colour separation by Keenes, Andover
Printed and bound by Leo Paper Products, China

A CIP catalogue record for this book is available from the British Library.

ISBN 978-0-7495-5704-1

Published by AA Publishing, a trading name of Automobile Association Developments Limited, whose registered office is Fanum House, Basing View, Basingstoke, Hampshire RG21 4EA. Registered number 1878835.

A03145
Mapping in this title produced from map data supplied by Global Mapping, Brackley, UK. Copyright © Global Mapping/Borch GmbH Publishing
Transport map © Communicarta Ltd, UK

The Automobile Association would like to thank the following photographers, companies and picture libraries for their assistance in the preparation of this book.

Abbreviations for the picture credits are as follows – (t) top; (b) bottom; (c) centre; (l) left; (r) right; (AA) AA World Travel Library.

Front cover © ImageState/Alamy; **back cover** (i) Lowe Art Museum; (ii) AA/C Sawyer; (iii) AA/L Provo; (iv) AA/P Bennett; **1** Greater Miami Convention & Visitors Bureau; **2/3t** Greater Miami Convention & Visitors Bureau; **4/5t** Greater Miami Convention & Visitors Bureau; **4tl** AA/L Provo; **5** Greater Miami Convention & Visitors Bureau; **6/7t** Greater Miami Convention & Visitors Bureau; **6c(i)** Photodisc; **6c(ii)** AA/D Lyons; **6c(iii)** AA/P Bennett; **6c(iv)** AA/P Bennett; **6b(i)** AA/P Bennett; **6b(ii)** Bass Museum of Art; **6b(iii)** Photodisc; **7c(i)** AA/P Bennett; **7c(ii)** Miami Science Museum; **7c(iii)** AA/J Davison; **7b(i)** AA/J Davison; **7b(ii)** AA/J Davison; **7b(iii)** © James Quine/Alamy; **8/9t** Greater Miami Convention & Visitors Bureau; **10/11t** Greater Miami Convention & Visitors Bureau; **10t** AA/L Provo; **10c** Greater Miami Convention & Visitors Bureau; **10b** AA/P Bennett; **10/11b** AA/J Davison; **11t** AA/P Bennett; **11c** Photodisc; **11b** AA/J Davison; **12/13t** Greater Miami Convention & Visitors Bureau; **13t** Greater Miami Convention & Visitors Bureau; **13c** Greater Miami Convention & Visitors Bureau; **13b** AA/J Davison; **14/15t** Greater Miami Convention & Visitors Bureau; **14t** Greater Miami Convention & Visitors Bureau; **14tc** AA/P Bennett; **14bc** AA/P Bennett; **14b** AA/P Bennett; **16/17t** Greater Miami Convention & Visitors Bureau; **16t** AA/P Bennett; **16tc** AA/K Paterson; **16bcr** © dk/Alamy; **16b** Image 100; **17t** AA/P Bennett; **17tc** AA/J Davison; **17cb** Brand X Pics; **17b** AA/P Bennett; **18t** Greater Miami Convention & Visitors Bureau; **18tr** AA/J A Tims; **18tcr** AA/J Davison; **18bcr** AA/J Davison; **18br** Greater Miami Convention & Visitors Bureau; **19t** Dacra © 2006 Red Square Inc. All Rights Reserved; **19tc** AA/J Davison; **19c** Lowe Art Museum; **19bc** AA/J Davison; **19b** AA/P Bennett; **20/21** AA/L Provo; **24l** Dacra; **24tr** Dacra; **24br** Dacra; **25t** Dacra; **25bl** Dacra RICHARD PATTERSON ©; **25br** Dacra © 2006 Red Square Inc. All Rights Reserved; **26l** © dk/Alamy; **26r** © Jeff Greenberg/Alamy; **27l** © Barry Lewis/Alamy; **27r** AA/P Bennett; **28l** AA/P Bennett; **28tr** AA/P Bennett; **28br** AA/P Bennett; **29t** AA/P Bennett; **29bl** Miami Art Museum; **29br** Miami Art Museum; **30l** Miami Children's Museum; **30c** Miami Children's Museum, Dana Bowden; **30r** Miami Children's Museum, Dana Bowden; **31l** AA/P Bennett; **31r** AA/J Davison; **32/33** AA/J Davison; **32** © Danita Delimont/Alamy; **33l** AA/P Bennett; **33r** AA/P Bennett; **34t** AA/J Davison; **34bl** AA/L Provo; **34br** AA/P Bennett; **35** AA/J Davison; **36t** Photodisc; **37** Photodisc; **38** AA/L Provo; **39** AA/P Bennett; **40t** AA/P Bennett; **41** AA/J Davison; **44l** Sandro Botticelli (Italian, 1444–1510) Domenico Ghirlandaio (Italian, 1449–1494) *The Coronation of the Virgin with Saints*, c. 1492, Collection Bass Museum of Art, gift of John and Johanna Bass; **44tr** Photo by Simon Hare, Bass Museum of Art; **44br** Bass Museum of Art; **45t** Bass Museum of Art; **45bl** Peter Paul Rubens and Studio (Flemish, 1577–1640) *The Flight of Lot and His Family from Sodom*, Collection Bass Museum of Art, gift of John and Johanna Bass; **45br** Photo by Peter Harholdt, Bass Museum of Art; **46l** AA/D Lyons; **46r** AA/P Bennett; **47l** © Jeff Greenberg/Alamy; **47r** Greater Miami Convention & Visitors Bureau; **48t** AA/P Bennett; **48bl** AA/J Davison; **48br** AA/J Davison; **49tl** AA/P Bennett; **49bl** AA/P Bennett; **49r** AA/P Bennett; **50tl** The Wolfsonian-Florida International University, Miami Beach, Florida; **50tc** Sculpture, *Profilo continuo del Duce* [Continuous Profile of Mussolini], 1933, Renato Bertelli (Italian, 1900–74); Photo: Bruce White, The Wolfsonian-Florida International University, Miami Beach, Florida, The Mitchell Wolfson, Jr. Collection; **50tr** The Wolfsonian-Florida International University, Miami Beach, Florida; **51t** AA/P Bennett; **51bl** AA/J Davison; **51br** AA/P Bennett; **52t** AA/P Bennett; **52b** © Jack Sullivan/Alamy; **53** AA/L Provo; **54** AA/J Davison; **55** Photodisc; **56** Photodisc; **57** AA/P Bennett; **58** AA/P Bennett; **59** AA/P Bennett; **60** AA/P Bennett; **61** © Emma Stanford; **64l** AA/J Davison; **64r** AA/P Bennett; **65l** © Emma Stanford; **65r** © Emma Stanford; **66l** Lowe Art Museum, Tatiana Parcero, Mexico, b. 1967, *Cartografia Interior #43*, 1996 lambda print and acetate, museum purchase through funds from Friends of Art, © 1996 Tatiana Parcero; **66tr** Lowe Art Museum; **66br** Lowe Art Museum; **67tl** Lowe Art Museum; **67bl** Lowe Art Museum; **67r** Standing Priest Stela Late Classic period (AD 600–900) Maya (Mexico [Southern Campeche] or Guatemala), museum purchase and partial gift of May Cassard, Lowe Art Museum; **68l** AA/P Bennett; **68r** AA/P Bennett; **69l** AA/J Davison; **69r** AA/P Bennett; **70t** AA/L Provo; **70bl** AA/P Bennett; **70br** AA/J Davison; **71** Photodisc; **72** © Jeff Greenberg/Alamy; **73** AA/P Bennett; **74** Photodisc; **75** AA/P Bennett; **78l** AA/J Davison; **78r** Florida Department of Environmental Protection; **79l** AA/P Bennett; **79r** AA/P Bennett; **80l** AA/J Davison; **80r** AA/J Davison; **81l** Miami Science Museum; **81r** AA/J Davison; **82l** AA/J Davison; **82tr** AA/J Davison; **82br** AA/L Provo; **83t** AA/P Bennett; **83bl** AA/J Davison; **83br** AA/D Lyons; **84/85** AA/P Bennett; **84bl** AA/P Bennett; **84br** AA/P Bennett; **85b** AA/L Provo; **86** AA/J Davison; **87** AA/J Davison; **88** AA/L Provo; **89** AA/L Provo; **90** Photodisc; **91** AA/L Provo; **94t** AA/J A Tims; **94bl** AA/J A Tims; **94br** © Florida Images/Alamy; **95l** © FL Stock/Alamy; **95r** AA/J A Tims; **96l** AA/P Bennett; **96r** AA/J Davison; **97l** AA/P Bennett; **97r** AA/P Bennett; **98** AA/J Davison; **98/99t** AA/J Davison; **98/99b** AA/J Davison; **99** Greater Miami Convention & Visitors Bureau; **100/101** AA/J Davison; **100bl** AA/J Davison; **100br** AA/J Davison; **101** AA/N Setchfield; **102** AA/L Provo; **103** AA/J Davison; **104** AA/J A Tims; **105** AA/L Provo; **106t** AA/P Bennett; **106b** Photodisc; **107** AA/P Bennett; **108/109t** AA/C Sawyer; **108tr** AA/J Davison; **108tc** AA/P Bennett; **108bcr** AA/P Bennett; **108br** AA/J Davison; **110/111** AA/C Sawyer; **112** AA/C Sawyer; **113** AA/P Bennett; **114/115** AA/P Bennett; **116/117** AA/P Bennett; **117** AA/P Bennett; **118/119** AA/P Bennett; **120** MRI Bankers' Guide to Foreign Currency, Houston, USA; **120/121** AA/P Bennett; **122/123** AA/P Bennett; **124/125** AA/P Bennett; **124bl** AA/P Bennett; **124bc** Mary Evans Picture Library; **124br** AA/P Bennett; **125bl** Greater Miami Convention & Visitors Bureau; **125bc** AA/P Bennett; **125br** Mary Evans Picture Library

Every effort has been made to trace the copyright holders, and we apologise in advance for any accidental errors. We would be happy to apply the corrections in any following edition of this publication.